The Trifle

Frederick Orin Bartlett

Alpha Editions

This edition published in 2024

ISBN : 9789362094704

Design and Setting By
Alpha Editions
www.alphaedis.com
Email - info@alphaedis.com

As per information held with us this book is in Public Domain.
This book is a reproduction of an important historical work. Alpha Editions uses the best technology to reproduce historical work in the same manner it was first published to preserve its original nature. Any marks or number seen are left intentionally to preserve its true form.

Contents

CHAPTER I THE TROUBLE WITH MONTE .... - 1 -
CHAPTER II THE TROUBLE WITH MARJORY .... - 6 -
CHAPTER III A SUMMONS .... - 14 -
CHAPTER IV A PROPOSAL .... - 21 -
CHAPTER V PISTOLS .... - 25 -
CHAPTER VI GENDARMES AND ETHER .... - 33 -
CHAPTER VII THE ADVANTAGES OF BEING SHOT ...... - 39 -
CHAPTER VIII DRAWBACKS OF RECOVERY .... - 46 -
CHAPTER IX BLUE AND GOLD .... - 56 -
CHAPTER X THE AFFAIR AT MAXIM'S .... - 64 -
CHAPTER XI A CANCELED RESERVATION .... - 72 -
CHAPTER XII A WEDDING JOURNEY .... - 78 -
CHAPTER XIII A WEDDING JOURNEY (*continued*) .... - 85 -
CHAPTER XIV THE BRIDE RUNS AWAY .... - 91 -
CHAPTER XV IN THE DARK .... - 97 -
CHAPTER XVI A WALK ON THE QUAY .... - 103 -
CHAPTER XVII JUST MONTE .... - 108 -
CHAPTER XVIII PETER .... - 113 -
CHAPTER XIX AN EXPLANATION .... - 117 -
CHAPTER XX PAYING LIKE A MAN .... - 125 -
CHAPTER XXI BACK TO SCHEDULE .... - 134 -
CHAPTER XXII A CONFESSION .... - 142 -
CHAPTER XXIII LETTERS .... - 147 -
CHAPTER XXIV THE BLIND SEE .... - 155 -
CHAPTER XXV SO LONG .... - 167 -
CHAPTER XXVI FREEDOM .... - 172 -

CHAPTER XXVII WAR .... - 183 -
CHAPTER XXVIII THE CORNICE ROAD .... - 188 -
CHAPTER XXIX BENEATH THE STARS .... - 194 -

CHAPTER I
THE TROUBLE WITH MONTE

For a man to keep himself consistently amused for ten years after his graduation from college, even with an inheritance to furnish ample financial assistance, suggests a certain quality of genius. This much Monte Covington had accomplished—accomplished, furthermore, without placing himself under obligations of any sort to the opposite sex. He left no trail of broken hearts in his wake. If some of the younger sisters of the big sisters took the liberty of falling in love with him secretly and in the privacy of their chambers, that was no fault of his, and did neither them nor him the slightest harm.

Such minor complications could not very well be avoided, because, discreet as Monte tried to be, it was not possible for him to deny certain patent facts, to wit: that he was a Covington of Philadelphia; that he was six feet tall and light-haired; that he had wonderfully decent blue eyes; that he had a straight nose; that he had the firm mouth and jaws of an Arctic explorer; that he had more money than he knew what to do with; and that he was just old enough to be known as a bachelor without in the slightest looking like one.

At the point where the older sisters gave him up as hopeless, he came as a sort of challenge to the younger.

This might have proved dangerous for him had it not been for his schedule, which did not leave him very long in any one place and which kept him always pretty well occupied. By spending his winters at his New York club until after the holidays; then journeying to Switzerland for the winter sports; then to Nice for tennis; then to Paris for a month of gay spring and the Grand Prix; and so over to England for a few days in London and a month of golf along the coast—he was able to come back refreshed to his camp in the Adirondacks, there to fish until it was time to return to Cambridge for the football season, where he found himself still useful as a coach in the art of drop-kicking.

The fact that he could get into his old football togs without letting out any strings or pulling any in, and could even come through an occasional scrimmage without losing his breath, was proof that he kept himself in good condition.

It was not until his eleventh trip that Monte became aware of certain symptoms which seemed to hint that even as pleasant a cycle as his could not be pursued indefinitely. At Davos he first noted a change. Though he took the curves in the long run with a daring that proved his eye to be as quick and his nerves as steady as ever, he was restless.

Later, when he came to Nice, it was with a listlessness foreign to him. In the first place, he missed Edhart, the old maître d'hôtel who for a decade had catered to his primitive American tastes in the matter of foodstuffs with as much enthusiasm as if he had been a Parisian epicure.

The passing of Edhart did more to call Monte's attention to the fact that in his own life a decade had also passed than anything else could possibly have done. Between birthdays there is only the lapse each time of a year; but between the coming and going of the maître d'hôtel there was a period of ten years, which with his disappearance seemed to vanish. Monte was twenty-two when he first came to Nice, and now he was thirty-two. He became thirty-two the moment he was forced to point out to the new management his own particular table in the corner, and to explain that, however barbarous the custom might appear, he always had for breakfast either a mutton chop or a beefsteak. Edhart had made him believe, even to last year, that in this matter and a hundred others he was merely expressing the light preferences of a young man. Now, because he was obliged to emphasize his wishes by explicit orders, they became the definite likes and dislikes of a man of middle age.

For relief Monte turned to the tennis courts, and played so much in the next week that he went stale and in the club tournament put up the worst game of his life. That evening, in disgust, he boarded the train for Monte Carlo, and before eleven o'clock had lost five thousand francs at roulette—which was more than even he could afford for an evening's entertainment that did not entertain. Without waiting for the croupier to rake in his last note, Monte hurried out and, to clear his head, walked all the way back to Nice along the Cornice Road. Above him, the mountains; below, the blue Mediterranean; while the road hung suspended between them like a silver ribbon. Yet even here he did not find content.

Monte visited the rooms every evening for the next three days; but, as he did not play again and found there nothing more interesting than the faces, or their counterparts, which he had seen for the past ten years, the programme grew stupid.

So, really, he had no alternative but Paris, although it was several weeks ahead of his schedule. As a matter of fact, it was several weeks too early. The city was not quite ready for him. The trees in the Champs Élysées were in much the condition of a lady half an hour before an expected caller. The broad vista to the triumphal arches was merely the setting for a few nurses and their charges. The little iron tables were so deserted that they remained merely little iron tables.

Of course the boulevards were as always; but after a night or two before the Café de la Paix he had enough. Even with fifty thousand people passing in review before him, he was not as amused as he should have been. He sipped his black coffee as drowsily as an old man.

In an effort to rouse himself, he resolved to visit the cafés upon Montmartre, which he had outgrown many years ago. That night he climbed the narrow stairs to l'Abbaye. It was exactly as it had been—a square room bounded by long seats before tables. Some two dozen young ladies of various nationalities wandered about the center of the room, trying their best, but with manifest effort, to keep pace to the frenzied music of an orchestra paid to keep frenzied. A half-dozen of the ladies pounced upon Monte as he sat alone, and he gladly turned over to them the wine he purchased as the price of admission. Yvonne, she with the languid Egyptian eyes, tried to rouse the big American. Was it that he was bored? Possibly it was that, Monte admitted. Then another bottle of wine was the proper thing. So he ordered another bottle, and to the toast Yvonne proposed, raised his glass. But the wine did him no good, and the music did him no good, and Yvonne did him no good. The place had gone flat. Whatever he needed, it was nothing l'Abbaye had to offer.

Covington went out into the night again, and, though the music from a dozen other cafés called him to come in and forget, he continued down the hill to the boulevard, deaf to the gay entreaties of the whole city. It was clear that he was out of tune with Paris.

As he came into the Place de l'Opera he ran into the crowd pouring from the big gray opera house, an eager, voluble crowd that jostled him about as if he were an intruder. They had been warmed by fine music and stirred by the great passions of this mimic world, so that the women clung more tightly to the arms of their escorts.

Covington, who had fallen back a little to watch them pass, felt strangely isolated. They hurried on without seeing him, as if he were merely some spectral bystander. Yet the significant fact was not that a thousand strangers should pass him without being aware of his presence, but that he himself should notice their indifference. It was not like him.

Ordinarily it was exactly what he would desire. But to-night he was in an unusual mood—a mood that was the culmination of a restlessness covering an entire month. But what the deuce was the name and cause of it? He could no longer attribute it to the fact that he had gone stale physically, because he had now had a rest of several weeks. It was not that he was bored; those who are bored never stop to ask themselves why they are bored or they would not be bored. It was not that he was homesick, because, strictly speaking, he had no home. A home seems to involve the female element and some degree of permanence. This unrest was something new—something, apparently, that had to do vaguely with the fact that he was thirty-two. If Edhart—

Impatiently he started again for his hotel. This confoundedly good-natured, self-satisfied crowd moving in couples irritated him. At that moment a tall, slender girl turned, hesitated, then started toward him. He did not recognize her at first, but the mere fact that she came toward him—that any one came toward him—quickened his pulse. It brought him back instantly from the shadowy realm of specters to the good old solid earth. It was he, Covington, who was standing there.

Then she raised her eyes—dark eyes deep as trout pools; steady, confident, but rather sad eyes. They appeared to be puzzled by the eagerness with which he stepped forward and grasped her hand.

"Marjory!" he exclaimed. "I did n't know you were in Paris!"

She smiled—a smile that extended no farther than the corners of her perfect mouth.

"That's to excuse yourself for not looking me up, Monte?"

She had a full, clear voice. It was good to hear a voice that he could recognize.

"No," he answered frankly. "That's honest. I thought you were somewhere in Brittany. But are you bound anywhere in particular?"

"Only home."

"Still living on the Boulevard Saint-Germain?"

She nodded.

"Number forty-three?"

He was glad he was able to remember that number.

"Number sixty-four," she corrected.

They had been moving toward the Metro station, and here she paused.

"There is no need for you to come with me," she said. "But I'd like to have you drop in for tea some afternoon—if you have time."

The strangers were still hurrying past him—to the north, the south, the east, the west. Men and women were hurrying past, laughing, intent upon themselves, each with some definite objective in mind. He himself was able to smile with them now. Then she held out her gloved hand, and he felt alone again.

"I may accompany you home, may I not?" he asked eagerly.

"If you wish."

Once again she raised her eyes with that expression of puzzled interest. This was not like Monte. Of course he would accompany her home, but that he should seem really to take pleasure in the prospect—that was novel.

"Let me call a taxi," he said. "I'm never sure where these French undergrounds are going to land me."

"They are much quicker," she suggested.

"There is no hurry," he answered.

With twenty-four hours a day on his hands, he was never in a hurry.

Instead of giving to the driver the number sixty-four Boulevard Saint-Germain, he ordered him to forty-seven Rue Saint-Michel, which is the Café d'Harcourt.

It had suddenly occurred to Monte what the trouble was with him. He was lonesome.

CHAPTER II
THE TROUBLE WITH MARJORY

She was surprised when the car stopped before the café, and mildly interested.

"Do you mind?" he asked.

"No, Monte."

She followed him through the smoke and chatter to one of the little dining-rooms in the rear where the smoke and chatter were somewhat subdued. There Henri removed their wraps with a look of frank approval. It was rather an elaborate dinner that Monte ordered, because he remembered for the first time that he had not yet dined this evening. It was also a dinner of which he felt Edhart would thoroughly approve, and that always was a satisfaction.

"Now," he said to the girl, as soon as Henri had left, "tell me about yourself."

"You knew about Aunt Kitty?" she asked.

"No," he replied hesitatingly, with an uneasy feeling that it was one of those things that he should know about.

"She was taken ill here in Paris in February, and died shortly after we reached New York," she explained.

What Covington would have honestly liked to do was to congratulate her. Stripping the situation of all sentimentalism, the naked truth remained that she had for ten years given up her life utterly to her aunt—had almost sold herself into slavery. Ostensibly this Aunt Kitty had taken the girl to educate, although she had never forgiven her sister for having married Stockton; had never forgiven her for having had this child, which had cost her life; had never forgiven Stockton for losing in business her sister's share of the Dolliver fortune.

Poor old Stockton—he had done his best, and the failure killed him. It was Chic Warren who had told Covington the pitiful little tale. Chic always spoke of the aunt as "the Vamp.," the abbreviation, as he explained, being solely out of respect to her gray hairs. Marjory had received her education, to be sure; but she had paid for it in the only coin she had—the best of her young self from seventeen to twenty-seven. The only concession the aunt had ever made was to allow her niece to study art in Paris this last year.

"I have n't heard from Chic since Christmas," he explained; "so I did n't know. Then you are back here in Paris—alone?"

Unconsciously he had emphasized that word "alone."

"Why not?" she asked directly.

She held her head a bit high, as if in challenge.

"Nothing; only—"

He did not finish. He could not very well tell her that she was too confoundedly good-looking to be alone in Paris. Yet that was what he thought, in spite of his belief that, of all the women he had ever met, she was the best able to be alone anywhere. There were times when he had sat beside her, not feeling sure that he was in the same room with her: it was as if he were looking at her through plate-glass. To-night, however, it was not like that. She looked like a younger sister of herself.

"Still painting?" he inquired.

"As much as they will let me."

"They?"

She leaned forward with a frown, folding her arms upon the table.

"What is the matter with men?" she demanded. "Why won't they believe a woman when she tells the truth?"

He was somewhat startled by the question, and by her earnestness.

"Just what do you mean?"

"Why can't they leave a woman alone?"

It was clear that he was not expected to answer, and so, with her permission, he lighted a cigarette and waited with considerable interest for her to go on.

For a moment she studied him, as if wondering if it were worth while to continue her confidence. Her acquaintance with Monte dated back ten years, when, as a girl of seventeen, she had met him on one of his rare week-end visits to the Warrens. She was then fresh from finishing school, and he was one of the very few men she had been allowed to meet in any more intimate way than merely to shake hands with in passing. She had been tremendously impressed. She could smile at it now. But, really, she had been like one of the younger sisters, and for a year or so after that he had been to her a sort of vague knight errant.

It was three years ago that her aunt had begun to travel with her, and after that she had seen Monte not oftener than once or twice a year, and then for scarcely more than a greeting and good-bye. On the other hand, Mrs. Warren had always talked and written to her a great deal about him. Chic and he had been roommates in college, and ever since had kept in close touch with each other by letter. The trivial gossip of Monte's life had always been passed on to Marjory, so that she had really for these last few years been following his movements and adventures month by month, until she felt in almost as intimate contact with him as with the Warrens. She had reason to think that, in turn, her movements were retailed to Monte. The design was obvious—and amusing.

On the whole, Marjory concluded that it was not especially worth while to burden him with her troubles; and yet, it was just because of that she was inclined to continue—in, however, a less serious mood. Monte had so few burdens of his own. That odd little smile—scarcely more than the ghost of a smile—returned to the corners of her mouth.

"To-night," she said, "I ran away from Teddy Hamilton, for all the world like a heroine of melodrama. Do you know Teddy?"

"Yes," he answered slowly, "I do."

He refrained with difficulty from voicing his opinion of the man, which he could have put into three words—"the little beast." But how did it happen that she, of all women, had been thrown into contact with this pale-faced Don Juan of the New York music-halls and Paris cafés?

"I lent Marie, my maid, one of my new hats and a heavy veil," she went on. "She came out and stepped into a taxi, with instructions to keep driving in a circle of a mile. Teddy followed in another machine. And"—she paused to look up and smile—"for all I know, he may still be following her round and round. I came on to the opera."

"Kind of tough on Marie," he commented, with his blue eyes reflecting a hearty relish of the situation.

"Marie will undoubtedly enjoy a nap," she said. "As for Teddy—well, he is generally out of funds, so I hope he may get into difficulties with the driver."

"He won't," declared Monte. "He'll probably end by borrowing a *pour-boire* of the driver."

She nodded.

"That is possible. He is very clever."

"The fact that he is still out of jail—" began Monte.

Then he checked himself. He was not a man to talk about other men—even about one so little of a man as Teddy Hamilton.

"Tell me what you know of him," she requested.

"I'd rather not," he answered.

"Is he as bad as that?" she queried thoughtfully. "But what I don't understand is why—why, then, he can sing like a white-robed choir-boy."

Monte looked serious.

"I've heard him," he admitted. "But it was generally after he had been sipping absinthe rather heavily. His specialty is 'The Rosary.'"

"And the barcarole from the 'Contes d'Hoffmann.'"

"And little Spanish serenades," he added.

"But if he's all bad inside?"

She raised those deep, dark eyes as a child might. She had been for ten years like one in a convent.

Covington shook his head.

"I can't explain it," he said. "Perhaps, in a way, it's because of that—because of the contrast. But I 've heard him do it. I 've heard him make a room full of those girls on Montmartre stop their dancing and gulp hard. But where—"

"Did I meet him?" she finished. "It was on the boat coming over this last time. You see— I 'm talking a great deal about myself."

"Please go on."

He had forgotten that her face was so young. The true lines of her features were scarcely more than sketched in, though that much had been done with a sure hand. Whatever was to come, he thought, must be added. There would be need of few erasures. Up to a certain point it was the face of any of those young women of gentle breeding that he met when at home—the inheritance of the best of many generations.

As she was sitting now, her head slightly turned, the arch of one brow blended in a perfect curve into her straight, thin nose. But the mouth and chin—they were firmer than one might have expected. If, not knowing her, he had seen her driving in the Bois or upon Rotten Row, he would have been curious about her title. It had always seemed to him that she should by rights have been Her Royal Highness Something or Other.

This was due partly to a certain air of serene security and a certain aloofness that characterized her. He felt it to a lesser degree to-night than ever before, but he made no mistake. He might be permitted to admire those features as one admires a beautiful portrait, but somewhere a barrier existed. There are faces that reflect the soul; there are faces that hide the soul.

"Please go on," he repeated, as she still hesitated.

She was trying to explain why it was that she was tempted at all to talk about herself to-night. Perhaps it was because she had been so long silent—for many years silent. Perhaps it was because Monte was so very impersonal that it was a good deal like talking out loud to herself, with the advantage of being able to do this without wondering if she were losing her wits. Then, too, after Teddy, Monte's straight-seeing blue eyes freshened her thoughts like a clean north wind. She always spoke of Monte as the most American man she knew; and by that she meant something direct and honest—something four-square.

"I met Teddy on the boat," she resumed. "I was traveling alone because—well, just because I wanted to be alone. You know, Aunt Kitty was very good to me, but I'd been with her every minute for more than ten years, and so I wanted to be by myself a little while. Right after she died, I went down to the farm—her farm in Connecticut—and thought I could be alone there. But—she left me a great deal of money, Monte."

Somehow, she could speak of such a thing to him. She was quite matter-of-fact about it.

"It was a great deal too much," she went on. "I did n't mind myself, because I could forget about it; but other people—they made me feel like a rabbit running before the hounds. Some one put the will in the papers, and people I'd never heard of began to write to me—dozens of them. Then men with all sorts of schemes—charities and gold mines and copper mines and oil wells and I don't know what all, came down there to see me: down there to the little farm, where I wanted to be alone. Of course, I could be out to them; but even then I was conscious that they were around. Some of them even waited until I ventured from the house, and waylaid me on the road.

"Then there were others—people I knew and could n't refuse to see without being rude. I felt," she said, looking up at Monte, "as if the world of people had suddenly all turned into men, and that they were hunting me. I could n't get away from them without locking myself up, and that was just the thing I did n't want to do. In a way, I 'd been locked up all my life. So I just packed my things and took the steamer without telling any one but my lawyer where I was going."

"It's too bad they wouldn't let you alone," said Monte.

"It was like an evil dream," she said. "I did n't know men were like that."

Monte frowned.

Of course, that is just what would happen to a young woman as good-looking as she, suddenly left alone with a fortune. Her name, without a doubt, was on the mailing list of every promoter from New York to San Francisco. It was also undoubtedly upon the list of every man and woman who could presume an acquaintance with her. She had become fair game.

"Then on the boat I met Teddy," she went on. "It was difficult not to meet him."

He nodded.

"I did n't mind so much at first; he was interesting."

"Yes, he's that," admitted Monte.

"And he was very pleasant until—he began to make love to me."

If Monte knew Teddy Hamilton, this happened about the third day.

"That was very annoying," she said reminiscently. "It was annoying, not only because of Teddy, but in itself. In some ways he did it very nicely—especially when he sang in the moonlight. I suppose it was my fault that I gave him the opportunity. I could have kept myself in my stateroom, or I could have played bridge with the elderly ladies in the cabin. But, you see, that's what Aunty always made me do, and I did want to get out. I did enjoy Teddy up to that point. But I did not want to fall in love with him, or with any one else. I suppose I 'm too selfish—too utterly and completely selfish."

"To—er—to fall in love?" he questioned.

"Yes. Oh, as long as I'm making you my father confessor, I may as well be thorough." She smiled.

Monte leaned forward with sudden interest. Here was a question that at odd moments had disturbed his own peace of mind. It was Chic Warren who had first told him that in remaining a bachelor he was leading an utterly selfish life.

"Does a distaste for falling in love necessarily go back to selfishness?" he asked. "Is n't it sometimes merely a matter of temperament?"

"And temperament," she asked, "is what?"

That was altogether too abstract a problem for Monte to discuss. Yet he had his own ideas.

"It's the way you're made," he suggested.

"I doubt it, Monte," she answered. "I think it's rather the way you make yourself; because I imagine that, to start with, we are all made a good deal alike. It's just what you 'd rather do."

"And you'd rather paint?"

She considered a moment. It was as if she were trying at this time to be very honest with herself.

"I'd rather be free to paint or not," she declared. "While Aunty was alive, to paint seemed to be the only way to be free. It gave me the excuse for coming here, for getting away a few hours a day. Now—well, just to be free seems enough. I don't suppose a man knows how a woman hungers for that—for just sheer, elemental freedom."

He did not. He supposed that freedom was what women enjoyed from birth—like queens. He supposed they even had especial opportunities in that direction, and that most men were in the nature of being their humble servitors.

"It is n't that I want to do anything especially proper or improper," she hastened to assure him. "I have n't either the cravings or the ambitions of the new woman. That, again, is where I 'm selfish. I'd like to be"—she spoke hesitatingly—"I'd like to be just like you, Monte."

"Like me?" he exclaimed in surprise.

"Free to do just what I want to do—nothing particularly good, nothing particularly bad; free to go here or go there; free to live my own life; free to be free."

"Well," he asked, "what's to prevent?"

"Teddy Hamilton—and the others," she answered. "In a way, they take the place of Aunty. They won't let me alone. They won't believe me when I tell them I don't want them around. They seem to assume that, just because I'm not married— Oh, they are stupid, Monte!"

Henri, who had been stealing in with course after course, refilled the glasses. He smiled discreetly as he saw her earnest face.

"What you need," suggested Monte, "is a sort of chaperon or secretary."

She shook her head.

"Would you like one yourself?" she demanded.

"It would be a good deal of a nuisance," he admitted; "but, after all—"

"I won't have it!" she burst out. "It would spoil everything. It would be like building one's own jail and employing one's own jailer. I could n't stand that. I 'd rather be annoyed as I am than be annoyed by a chaperon."

She was silent a moment, and then she exclaimed:

"Why, I'd almost rather marry Teddy! I'd feel freer—honestly, I think I 'd feel freer with a husband than a chaperon."

"Oh, see here!" protested Monte. "You must n't do that."

"I don't propose to," she answered quietly.

"Then," he said, "the only thing left is to go away where Teddy and the others can't find you."

"Where?" she asked with interest.

"There are lots of little villages in Switzerland."

She shook her head.

"And along the Riviera."

"I love the little villages," she replied. "I love them here and at home. But it's no use."

She smiled. There was something pathetic about that smile—something that made Covington's arm muscles twitch.

"I should n't even have the aid of the taxis in the little villages," she said.

Monte leaned back.

"If they only had here in Paris a force of good, honest Irish cops instead of these confounded gendarmes," he mused.

She looked her astonishment at the irrelevant observation.

"You see," he explained, "it might be possible then to lay for Teddy H. some evening and—argue with him."

"It's nice of you, Monte, to think of that," she murmured.

Monte was nice in a good many ways.

"The trouble is, they lack sentiment, these gendarmes," he concluded. "They are altogether too law-abiding."

CHAPTER III
A SUMMONS

Monte himself had sometimes been accused of lacking sentiment; and yet, the very first thing he did when starting for his walk the next morning was to order a large bunch of violets to be sent to number sixty-four Boulevard Saint-Germain. Then, at a somewhat faster pace than usual, he followed the river to the Jardin des Tuileries, and crossed there to the Avenue des Champs Élysées into the Bois.

He walked as confidently as if overnight his schedule had again been put in good running order; for, overnight, spring had come, and that was what his schedule called for in Paris. The buds, which until now had hesitated to unfold, trembled forth almost before his eyes under the influence of a sun that this morning blazed in a turquoise sky. Perhaps they had hurried a trifle to overtake Monte.

With his shoulders well back, filling his lungs deep with the perfumed morning air, he swung along with a hearty, self-confident stride that caused many a little nursemaid to turn and look at him again.

He had sent her violets; and yet, except for the fact that he had never before sent her flowers, he could not rightly be accused of sentimentalism. He had acted on the spur of the moment, remembering only the sad, wistful smile with which she had bade him good-night when she stood at the door of the *pension*. Or perhaps he had been prompted by the fact that she was in Paris alone.

Until now it had never been possible to dissociate her completely from Aunt Kitty. Marjory had never had a separate existence of her own. To a great many people she had never been known except as Miss Dolliver's charming niece, although to Monte she had been known more particularly as a young friend of the Warrens. But, even in this more intimate capacity, he had always been relieved of any sense of responsibility because of this aunt. Wherever he met her, there was never any occasion for him to put himself out to be nice to her, because it was always understood that she could never leave Aunt Kitty even for an evening. This gave him a certain sense of security. With her he never was forced to consider either the present or the future.

Last night it had been almost like meeting her for the first time alone. It was as if in all these years he had known her only through her photograph, as one knows friends of one's friends about whom one has for long heard a great deal, without ever meeting them face to face. From the moment he first saw her in the Place de l'Opera she had made him conscious of her as, in another way, he had always been conscious of Edhart. The latter, until his death, had always remained in Monte's outer consciousness like a fixed point. Because he was so permanent, so unchanging, he dominated the rest of Monte's schedule as the north star does the mariner's course.

Each year began when Edhart bade him a smiling au revoir at the door of the Hôtel des Roses; and that same year did not end, but began again, when the matter of ten or eleven months later Monte found Edhart still at the door to greet him. So it was always possible, the year round, to think of Edhart as ever standing by the door smilingly awaiting him. This was very pleasant, and prevented Monte from getting really lonesome, and consequently from getting old. It was only in the last few weeks that he fully realized all that Edhart had done for him.

It was, in some ways, as if Edhart had come back to life again in Marjory. He had felt it the moment she had smilingly confided in him; he felt it still more when, after she bade him good-night, he had turned back into the city, not feeling alone any more. Now it was as if he were indebted to her for this morning walk, and for restoring to him his springtime Paris. It was for these things that he had sent her violets—because she had made him comfortable again. So, after all, his act had been one, not of sentimentalism, but of just plain gratitude.

Monte's objection to sentiment was not based upon any of the modern schools of philosophy, which deplore it as a weakness. He took his stand upon much simpler grounds: that, as far as he had been able to observe, it did not make for content. It had been his fate to be thrown in contact with a good deal of it in its most acute stages, because the route he followed was unhappily the route also followed by those upon their honeymoon. If what he observed was sentiment at its zenith, then he did not care for it. Bridegrooms made the poorest sort of traveling companions; and that, after all, was the supreme test of men. They appeared restless, dazed, and were continually looking at their watches. Few of them were able to talk intelligently or to play a decent game of bridge.

Perhaps, too, he had been unfortunate in the result of his observations of the same passion in its later stages; but it is certain that those were not inspiring, either. Chic Warren was an exception. He seemed fairly happy and normal, but Covington would never forget the night he spent there when Chic, Junior had the whooping-cough. He walked by Chic's side up and down the hall, up and down the hall, up and down the hall, with Chic a ghastly white and the sweat standing in beads upon his forehead. His own throat had tightened and he grew weak in the knees every time the rubber-soled nurse stole into sight. Every now and then he heard that gasping cough, and felt the spasmodic grip of Chic's fingers upon his arm. It was terrible; for weeks afterward Covington heard that cough.

At the end of an hour Covington turned back, wheeling like a soldier on parade. There had never seemed to him any reason why, when a man was entirely comfortable, as he was, he should take the risk of a change. He had told Chic as much when sometimes the latter, over a pipe, had introduced the subject. The last time, Chic had gone a little farther than usual.

"But, man alive!" Chic had exclaimed. "A day will come when you'll be sorry."

"I don't believe it," Monte answered.

Yet it was only yesterday that he had wandered over half Paris in search of something to bring his schedule back to normal. And he had found it—in front of the Opera House at eleven o'clock at night.

Monte strode into his hotel with a snap that made the little clerk glance up in surprise.

"Any mail for me?" he inquired.

"A telephone message, monsieur."

He handed Monte an envelope. It was not often that he received telephone messages. It read as follows:—

Can't you come over? Teddy was very angry about the taxi, and I think I shall leave Paris tonight. The flowers were beautiful.

Monte felt his breath coming fast.

"How long has this been waiting for me?" he demanded.

"A half-hour, monsieur."

He hurried out the door and into a taxi.

"Sixty-four Boulevard Saint-Germain—and hurry."

Leaving Paris? She had no right to do that. Edhart never left. That was the beauty of Edhart—that he remained stationary, so that he could always be found. He was quite sure that Edhart was too considerate even to die, could he have avoided it. Now Marjory was proposing to go and leave him here alone. He could not allow that. It was too early to quit Paris, anyway. It was only the first day of spring!

She came down into the gloomy *pension* reception-room looking as if she had already begun to assist Marie with the packing. Her hair had become loosened, and escaped in several places in black curls that gave her a distinctly girlish appearance. There was more color, too, in her cheeks; but it was the flush of excitement rather than the honest red that colored his own cheeks. She looked tired and discouraged. She sank into a chair.

"It was good of you to come, Monte," she said. "But I don't know why I should bother you with my affairs. Only—he was so disagreeable. He frightened me, for a moment."

"What did he do?" demanded Monte.

"He came here early, and when Marie told him I was out he said he would wait until I came back. So he sat down—right here. Then, every five minutes, he called Madame Courcy and sent her up with a note. I was afraid of a scene, because madame spoke of sending for the gendarmes."

"Why didn't you let her?"

"That would have made still more of a scene."

She was speaking in a weary, emotionless voice, like one who is very tired.

"So I came down and saw him," she said. "He was very melodramatic."

It seemed difficult for her to go on.

"Absinthe?" he questioned.

"I don't know. He wanted me to marry him at once. He drew a revolver and threatened to shoot himself—threatened to shoot me."

Monte clenched his fists.

"Good Lord!" he said softly. "That is going a bit far."

"Is it so men act—when they are in love?" she asked.

Monte started.

"I don't know. If it is, then they ought to be put in jail."

"If it is, it is most unpleasant," she said; "and I can't stand it, Monte. There is no reason why I should, is there?"

"No: if you can avoid it."

"That's the trouble," she frowned. "I've been quite frank with him. I told him that I did not want to marry him. I've told him that I could not conceive of any possible circumstances under which I would marry him. I've told him that in French and I 've told him that in English, and he won't believe me."

"The cad!" exclaimed Monte.

"It does n't seem fair," she mused. "The only thing I ask for is to be allowed to lead my life undisturbed, and he won't let me. There are others, too. I had five letters this morning. So all I can do is to run away again."

"To where?" asked Monte.

"You spoke of the little villages along the Riviera."

"Yes," he nodded. "There is the village of Étois—back in the mountains."

"Then I might go there. *C'est tout égal.*"

She shrugged her shoulders. (She had beautiful shoulders.)

"But look here. Supposing the—this Hamilton should follow you there?"

"Then I must move again."

Monte paced the room. Obviously this was not right. There was no reason why she should be continually hounded. Yet there seemed to be no way to prevent it.

He stopped in front of her. She glanced up—her eyes, even now, calm and deep as trout pools.

"I'll get hold of the beggar to-day," he said grimly.

She shook her head.

"Please not."

"But he's the one who must go away. If I could have a few minutes with him alone, I think perhaps I could make him see that."

"Please not," she repeated.

"What's the harm?"

"I don't think it would be safe—for either of you."

She raised her eyes as she said that, and for a moment Monte was held by them. Then she rose.

"After all, it's too bad for me to inflict my troubles on you," she said.

"I don't mind," he answered quickly. "Only—hang it all, there does n't seem to be anything I can do!"

"I guess there is n't anything any one can do," she replied helplessly.

"So you're going away?"

"To-night," she nodded.

"To Étois?"

"Perhaps. Perhaps to India. Perhaps to Japan."

It was the indefiniteness that Monte did not relish. Even as she spoke, it was as if she began to disappear; and for a second he felt again the full weight of his thirty-two years. He was perfectly certain that the moment she went he was going to feel alone—more alone than he had ever felt in his life.

It was in the nature of a hunch. Within twenty-four hours he would be wandering over Paris as he had wandered yesterday. That would not do at all. Of course, he could pack up and go on to England, but at the moment he felt that it would be even worse there, where all the world spoke English.

"Suppose I order young Hamilton to leave Paris?" he asked.

"But what right have you to order him to leave Paris?"

"Well, I can tell him he is annoying you and that I won't stand for it," he declared.

For a second her eyes grew mellow; for a second a more natural red flushed her cheeks.

"If you were only my big brother, now," she breathed.

Monte saw the point. His own cheeks turned a red to match hers.

"You mean he'll ask—what business you are of mine?"

"Yes."

And Monte would have no answer. He realized that. As a friend he had, of course, certain rights; but they were distinctly limited. It was, for instance, no business of his whether she went to Étois or Japan or India. By no stretch of the imagination could he make it his business—though it affected his whole schedule, though it affected her whole life. As a friend he would be justified, perhaps, in throwing young Hamilton out of the door if he happened to be around when the man was actually annoying her; but there was no way in which he could guard her against such annoyances in the future. He had no authority that extended beyond the moment; nor was it possible for Marjory herself to give him that authority. Young Hamilton, if he chose, could harry her around the world, and it would be none of Monte's business.

There was something wrong with a situation of that sort. If he had only been born her brother or father, or even a first cousin, then it might be possible to do something, because, if necessary, he could remain always at hand. He wondered vaguely if there were not some law that would make him a first cousin. He was on the point of suggesting it when a bell jangled solemnly in the hall.

The girl clutched his arm.

"I'm afraid he's come again," she gasped.

Monte threw back his shoulders.

"Fine," he smiled. "It could n't be better."

"But I don't want to see him! I won't see him!"

"There is n't the slightest need in the world of it," he nodded. "You go upstairs, and I'll see him."

But, clinging to his arm, she drew him into the hall and toward the stairs. The bell rang again—impatiently.

"Come," she insisted.

He tried to calm her.

"Steady! Steady! I promise you I won't make a scene."

"But he will. Oh, you don't know him. I won't have it. Do you hear? I won't have it."

To Madame Courcy, who appeared, she whispered:—

"Tell him I refuse to see him again. Tell him you will call the gendarmes."

"It seems so foolish to call in those fellows when the whole thing might be settled quietly right now," pleaded Monte.

He turned eagerly toward the door.

"If you don't come away, Monte," she said quietly, "I won't ever send for you again."

Reluctantly he followed her up the stairs as the bell jangled harshly, wildly.

CHAPTER IV
A PROPOSAL

Dejectedly, Monte seated himself upon a trunk in the midst of a scene of fluffy chaos. Marie had swooped in from the next room, seized one armful, and returned in consternation as her mistress stood poised at the threshold. Then, with her face white, Marjory closed the door and locked it.

"He's down there," she informed Monte.

Monte glanced at his watch.

"It's quarter of twelve," he announced. "I'll give him until twelve to leave."

Marjory crossed to the window and stared out at the sun-lighted street. It was very beautiful out there—very warm and gentle and peaceful. And at her back all this turmoil. Once again the unspoken cry that sprang to her lips was just this:—

"It is n't fair—it is n't fair!"

For ten years she had surrendered herself to Aunt Kitty—surrendered utterly the deep, budding years of her young womanhood. To the last minute she had paid her obligations in full. Then, at the moment she had been about to spread her long-folded wings and soar into the sunshine, this other complication had come. When the lawyer informed her of the fortune that was hers, she had caught her breath. It spelled freedom. Yet she asked for so little—for neither luxuries nor vanities; for just the privilege of leading for a space her own life, undisturbed by any responsibility.

Selfish? Yes. But she had a right to be selfish for a little. She had answered that question when Peter Noyes—Monte reminded her in many ways of Peter—had come down to her farm in Littlefield one Sunday. She had seen more of Peter than of any other man, and knew him to be honest. He had been very gentle with her, and very considerate; but she knew what was in his heart, so she had put the question to herself then and there. If she chose to follow the road to which he silently beckoned—the road to all those wonderful hopes that had surged in upon her at eighteen—she had only to nod. If she had let herself go, she could have loved Peter. Then—she drew back at so surrendering herself. It meant a new set of self-sacrifices. It meant, however hallowed, a new prison. Because, if she loved, she would love hard.

Monte glanced at his watch again.

"Five minutes gone! Have you seen him leave?"

"No, Monte," she answered.

He folded his arms resignedly.

"You don't really mean to act against my wishes, Monte?"

"If that's the only way of getting rid of him," he answered coolly.

"But don't you see—don't you understand that you will only make a scandal of it?" she said.

"What do you mean?"

"If he makes a scene it will be in the papers, and then—oh, well, they will ask by what right—"

"I'd answer I was simply ridding you of a crazy man."

"They would smile. Oh, I know them! Here in Paris they won't believe that a woman who is n't married—"

She stopped abruptly.

Monte's brows came together.

Here was the same situation that had confronted him a few minutes before. Not only had he no right, but if he assumed a right his claim might be misinterpreted. Undoubtedly Teddy himself would be the first to misinterpret it. It would be impossible for a man of his sort to think in any other direction. And then—well, such stories were easier to start than to stop.

Monte's lips came together. As far as he himself was concerned, he was willing to take the risk; but the risk was not his to take. As long as he found himself unable to devise any scheme by which he could, even technically, make himself over into her father, her brother, or even a first cousin, there appeared no possible way in which he could assume the right that would not make it a risk.

Except one way.

Here Monte caught his breath.

There was just one relationship open to him that would bestow upon him automatically the undeniable right to say to Teddy Hamilton anything that might occur to him—that would grant him fuller privileges, now and for as long as the relationship was maintained, than even that of blood.

To be sure, the idea was rather staggering. It was distinctly novel, for one thing, and not at all in his line, for another. This, however, was a crisis calling for staggering novelties if it could not be handled in the ordinary way. Ten minutes had already passed.

Monte walked slowly to Marjory's side. She turned and met his eyes. On the whole, he would have felt more comfortable had she continued looking out the window.

"Marjory," he said—"Marjory, will you marry me?"

She shrank away.

"Monte!"

"I mean it," he said. "Will you marry me?"

After the first shock she seemed more hurt than anything.

"You are n't going to be like the others?" she pleaded.

"No," he assured her. "That's why—well, that's why I thought we might arrange it."

"But I don't love you, Monte!" she exclaimed.

"Of course not."

"And you—you don't love me."

"That's it," he nodded eagerly.

"Yet you are asking me to marry you?"

"Just because of that," he said. "Don't you understand?"

She was trying hard to understand, because she had a great deal of faith in Monte and because at this moment she needed him.

"I don't see why being engaged to a man you don't care about need bother you at all," he ran on. "It's the caring that seems to make the trouble—whether you 're engaged or not. I suppose that's what ails Teddy."

She had been watching Monte's eyes; but she turned away for a second.

"Of course," he continued, "you can care—without caring too much. Can't people care in just a friendly sort of way?"

"I should think so, Monte," she answered.

"Then why can't people become engaged—in just a friendly sort of way?"

"It would n't mean very much, would it?"

"Just enough," he said.

He held out his hand.

"Is it a bargain?"

She searched his eyes. They were clean and blue.

"It's so absurd, Monte!" she gasped.

"You can call me, to yourself, your secretary," he suggested.

"No—not that."

"Then," he said, "call me just a *camarade de voyage*."

Her eyes warmed a trifle.

"I'll keep on calling you just Monte," she whispered.

And she gave him her hand.

CHAPTER V
PISTOLS

Evidently young Hamilton did not hear Monte come down the stairs, for he was sitting in a chair near the window, with his head in his hands, and did not move even when Monte entered the room.

"Hello, Hamilton," said Covington.

Hamilton sprang to his feet—a shaking, ghastly remnant of a man. He had grown thinner and paler than when Covington last saw him. But his eyes—they held Covington for a moment. They burned in their hollow sockets like two candles in a dark room.

"Covington!" gasped the man.

Then his eyes narrowed.

"What the devil you doing here?" he demanded.

"Sit down," suggested Monte. "I want to have a little talk with you."

It was physical weakness that forced Hamilton to obey.

Monte drew up a chair opposite him.

"Now," he said quietly, "tell me just what it is you want of Miss Stockton."

"What business is that of yours?" demanded Hamilton nervously.

Monte was silent a moment. Here at the start was the question Marjory had anticipated—the question that might have caused him some embarrassment had it not been so adequately provided for in the last few moments. As it was, he became conscious of a little glow of satisfaction which moderated his feelings toward young Hamilton considerably. He actually felt a certain amount of sympathy for him. After all, the little beggar was in bad shape.

But, even now, there was no reason, just yet, why he should make him his confidant. Secure in his position, he felt it was none of Hamilton's business.

"Miss Stockton and I are old friends," he answered.

"Then—she has told you?"

"She gave me to believe you made a good deal of an ass of yourself this morning," nodded Monte.

Hamilton sank back limply in his chair.

"I did," he groaned. "Oh, my God, I did!"

"All that business of waving a pistol—I did n't think you were that much of a cub, Hamilton."

"She drove me mad. I did n't know what I was doing."

"In just what way do you blame her?" inquired Monte.

"She would n't believe me," exclaimed Hamilton. "I saw it in her eyes. I could n't make her believe me."

"Believe what?"

Hamilton got to his feet and leaned against the wall. He was breathing rapidly, like a man in a fever.

Monte studied him with a curious interest.

"That I love her," gasped Hamilton. "She thought I was lying. I could n't make her believe it, I tell you! She just sat there and smiled—not believing."

"Good Lord!" said Monte. "You don't mean that you really do love her?"

Hamilton sprang with what little strength there was in him.

"Damn you, Covington—what do you think?" he choked.

Monte caught the man by the arms and forced him again into his chair.

"Steady," he warned.

Exhausted by his exertion, Hamilton sat there panting for breath, his eyes burning into Covington's.

"What I meant," said Monte, "was, do you love her with—with an honest-to-God love?"

When Hamilton answered this time, Covington saw what Marjory meant when she wondered how Hamilton could look like a white-robed choir-boy as he sang to her. He had grown suddenly calm, and when he spoke the red light in his eyes had turned to white.

"It's with all there is in me, Covington," he said.

The pity of it was, of course, that so little was left in him—that so much had been wasted, so much soiled, in the last few years. The wonder was that so much was left.

As Monte looked down at the man, he felt his own heart beating faster. He felt several other things that left him none too comfortable. Again that curious interest that made him want to listen, that held him with a weird fascination.

"Tell me about it," said Covington.

Hamilton sat up with a start. He faced Covington as if searching his soul.

"Do you believe me?" he demanded.

"Yes," answered Monte; "I think I do."

"Because—did you see a play in New York called 'Peter Grimm'?"

"I remember it," nodded Monte.

"It's been like that—like dying and coming back and trying to make people hear, and not being able to. I made an ass of myself until I met her. I know that. I'm not fit to be in the same room with her. I know that you can say nothing too bad about me—up to the day I met her. I would n't care what people said up to that day—if they'd only believe the rest; if she'd only believe the rest. I think I could stand it even if I knew she—she did not care for me—if only I could make her understand how much she means to me."

Monte looked puzzled.

"Just what does she mean to you?" he asked.

"All that's left in life," answered Hamilton. "All that's left to work for, to live for, to hope for. It's been like that ever since I saw her on the boat. I was coming over here to go the old rounds, and then—everything was changed. There was no place to go, after that, except where she went. I counted the hours at night to the time when the sun came up and I could see her again. I did n't begin to live until then; the rest of the time I was only waiting to live. Every time she came in sight it—it was as if I were resurrected, Covington; as if in the mean while I'd been dead. I thought at first I had a chance, and I planned to come back home with her to do things. I wanted to do big things for her. I thought I had a chance all the while, until she came here—until this morning. Then, when she only smiled—well, I lost my head."

"What was the idea back of the gun?" asked Monte.

Hamilton answered without bravado.

"I meant to end it for both of us; but I lost my nerve."

"Good Lord! You would have gone as far as that?"

"Yes," answered Hamilton wearily. "But I'm glad I fell down."

Monte passed his hand over his forehead. He could not fully grasp the meaning of a passion that led a man to such lengths as this. Why, the man had proposed murder—murder and suicide; and all because of this strange love of a woman. He had been driven stark raving mad because of it. He sat there now before him, an odd combination of craven weakness and giant strength because of it. In the face of such a revelation, Covington felt petty; he felt negative.

Less than ten minutes ago he himself had looked into the same eyes that had so stirred this man. He had seen nothing there particularly to disturb any one. They were very beautiful eyes, and the woman back of them was very beautiful. He had a feeling that, day in and day out for a great many years, they would remain beautiful. They had helped him last night to make the city his own; they had helped him this morning to recover his balance; they helped him now to see straight again.

But, after all, it was arrant nonsense for Hamilton to act like this. Admitting the man believed in himself,—and Covington believed that much,—he was, after all, Teddy Hamilton. The fact remained, even as he himself admitted, that he was not fit to be in the same room with her. It was not possible for a man in a month to cleanse himself of the accumulated mire of ten years.

Furthermore, that too was beside the point. The girl cared nothing about him. She particularly desired not to care about him or any one else. It was not consistent with her scheme of life. She had told him as much. It was this that had made his own engagement to her possible.

Monte rose from his chair and paced the room a moment. If possible, he wished to settle this matter once for all. On the whole, it was more difficult than he had anticipated. When he came down he had intended to dispose of it in five minutes. Suddenly he wheeled and faced Hamilton.

"It seems to me," he said, "that if a man loved a woman,—really loved her,—then one of the things he would be most anxious about would be to make her happy. Are you with me on that?"

Hamilton raised his head.

"Yes," he answered.

"Then," continued Monte, "it does n't seem to me that you are going about it in just the right way. Waving pistols and throwing fits—"

"I was mad, I tell you," Hamilton broke in.

"Admitting that," resumed Monte, "I should think the best thing you could do would be to go away and sober up."

"Go away?"

"I would. I'd go a long way—to Japan or India."

The old mad light came back to Hamilton's eyes.

"Did she ask you to tell me that?"

"No," answered Monte; "it is my own idea. Because, you see, if you don't go she'll have to."

"What do you mean?"

"Steady, now," warned Monte. "I mean just what I say. She can't stay here and let you camp in her front hall. Even Madame Courcy won't stand for that. So—why don't you get out, quietly and without any confusion?"

"That's your own suggestion?" said Hamilton, tottering to his feet.

"Exactly."

"Then," said Hamilton, "I'll see you in hell first. It's no business of yours, I say."

"But it is," said Monte.

"Tell me how it is," growled Hamilton.

"Why, you see," said Monte quietly, "Miss Stockton and I are engaged."

"You lie!" choked Hamilton. "You—"

Monte heard a deafening report, and felt a biting pain in his shoulder. As he staggered back he saw a pistol smoking in Hamilton's hand. Recovering, he threw himself forward on the man and bore him to the floor.

It was no very difficult matter for Monte to wrest the revolver from Hamilton's weak fingers, even with one arm hanging limp; but it was quite a different proposition to quiet Madame Courcy and Marie, who were screaming hysterically in the hall. Marjory, to be sure, was splendid; but even she could do little with madame, who insisted that some one had been murdered, even when it was quite obvious, with both men alive, that this was a mistake. To make matters worse, she had called up the police on the telephone, and at least a dozen gendarmes were now on their way.

The pain in Monte's arm was acute, and it hung from his shoulder as limply as an empty sleeve; but, fortunately, it was not bleeding a great deal,—or at least it was not messing things up,—and he was able, therefore, by always keeping his good arm toward the ladies, to conceal from them this disagreeable consequence of Hamilton's rashness.

Hamilton himself had staggered to his feet, and, leaning against the wall, was staring blankly at the confusion about him.

Monte turned to Marjory.

"Hurry out and get a taxi," he said. "We can't allow the man to be arrested."

"He tried to shoot—himself?" she asked.

"I don't believe he knows what he tried to do. Hurry, please."

As she went out, he turned to Marie.

"Help madame into her room," he ordered.

Madame did not want to go; but Monte impatiently grasped one arm and Marie the other, so madame went.

Then he came back to Hamilton.

"Madame has sent for the police. Do you understand?"

"Yes," Hamilton answered dully.

"And I have sent for a taxi. It depends on which gets here first whether you go to jail or not," said Monte.

Then he sat down in a chair, because his knees were beginning to feel weak.

Marjory was back in a minute, and when she came in Monte was on his feet again.

"It's at the door," she said.

At the sound of her voice Hamilton seemed to revive; but Monte had him instantly by the arm.

"Come on," he ordered.

He shoved the boy ahead a little as he passed Marjory, and turning, drew the revolver from his pocket. He did not dare take it with him, because he knew that in five minutes he would be unable to use it. Hamilton, on the other hand, might not be. He shoved it into her hand.

"Take it upstairs and hide it," he said. "Be careful with it."

"You're coming back here?" she asked quickly.

She thought his cheeks were very white.

"I can't tell," he answered. "But—don't worry."

He hurried Hamilton down the steps and pushed him into the car.

"To the Hôtel Normandie," he ordered the driver, as he stumbled in himself.

The bumping of the car hurt Monte's arm a good deal. In fact, with every bump he felt as if Hamilton were prodding his shoulder with a stiletto. Besides being unpleasant, this told rapidly on his strength, and that was dangerous. Above all things, he must remain conscious. Hamilton was quiet because he thought Monte still had the gun and was still able to use it; but let him sway, and matters would be reversed. So Monte gripped his jaws and bent his full energy to keeping control of himself until they crossed the Seine. It seemed like a full day's journey before he saw that the muddy waters were behind them. Then he ordered the driver to stop.

Hamilton's shifty eyes looked up.

"Hamilton," said Monte, "have you got it clear yet that—that Miss Stockton and I are engaged?"

Hamilton did not answer. His fingers were working nervously.

Monte, summoning all his strength, shook the fellow.

"Do you hear?" he called.

"Yes," muttered Hamilton.

"Then," said Monte, "I want you to get hold of the next point: that from now on you're to let her alone. Get that?"

Hamilton's lips began to twitch.

"Because if you come around bothering her any more," explained Monte, "I'll be there myself; and, believe me, you'll go out the door. And if you try any more gun-play—the little fellows will nail you next time. Sure as preaching, they'll nail you. That would be too bad for every one—for you and for her."

"How for her?" demanded Hamilton hoarsely.

"The papers," answered Monte. "And for you because—"

"I don't care what they do to me," growled Hamilton.

"I believe that," nodded Monte. "Do you know that I'm the one person on earth who is inclined to believe what you say?"

He saw Hamilton crouch as if to spring. Monte placed his left hand in his empty pocket.

"Steady," he warned. "There are still four shots left in that gun."

Hamilton relaxed.

"You don't care what the little fellows do to you," said Monte. "But you don't want to queer yourself any further with her, do you? Now, listen. She thinks you tried to shoot yourself. By that much I have a hunch she thinks the better of you."

Hamilton groaned,

"And because I believe what you told me about her," he ran on, fighting for breath—"just because—because I believe the shooting fits into that, I'm glad to—to have her think that little the better of you, Hamilton."

The interior of the cab was beginning to move slowly around in a circle. He leaned back his head a second to steady himself—his white lips pressed together.

"So—so—clear out," he whispered.

"You—you won't tell her?"

"No. But—clear out, quick."

Hamilton opened the cab door.

"Got any money?" inquired Monte.

"No."

Monte drew out his bill-book and handed it to Hamilton.

"Take what there is," he ordered.

Hamilton obeyed, and returned the empty purse.

"Remember," faltered Monte, his voice trailing off into an inaudible murmur, "we're engaged—Marjory and I—"

But Hamilton had disappeared. It was the driver who was peering in the door.

"Where next, monsieur?" he was saying.

"Normandie," muttered Monte.

The windows began to revolve in a circle before his eyes—faster and faster, until suddenly he no longer was conscious of the pain in his shoulder.

CHAPTER VI
GENDARMES AND ETHER

When the gendarmes came hurrying to sixty-four Boulevard Saint-Germain, Marjory was the only one in the house cool enough to meet them at the door. She quieted them with a smile.

"It is too bad, messieurs," she apologized, because it did seem too bad to put them to so much trouble for nothing. "It was only a disagreeable incident between friends, and it is closed. Madame Courcy lost her head."

"But we were told it was an assassination," the lieutenant informed her. He was a very smart-looking lieutenant, and he noticed her eyes at once.

"To have an assassination it is necessary to have some one assassinated, is it not?" inquired Marjory.

"But yes, certainly."

"Then truly it is a mistake, because the two gentlemen went off together in a cab."

The lieutenant took out a memorandum-book.

"Is that necessary?" asked Marjory anxiously.

"A report must be made."

"It was nothing, I assure you," she insisted. "It was what in America is called a false alarm."

"You are American?" inquired the lieutenant, twisting his mustache.

"It is a compliment to my French that you did not know," smiled Marjory.

It was also a compliment to the lieutenant that she smiled. At least, it was so that he interpreted it.

"The report is only a matter of routine," he informed her. "If mademoiselle will kindly give me her name."

"But the newspapers!" she exclaimed. "They make so much of so little."

"It will be a pleasure to see that the report is treated as confidential," said the lieutenant, with a bow.

So, as a matter of fact, after a perfunctory interview with madame and Marie, who had so far recovered themselves as to be easily handled by Marjory, the lieutenant and his men bowed themselves out and the incident was closed.

Marjory escorted them to the door, and then, a little breathless with excitement, went into the reception room a moment to collect herself.

The scene was set exactly as it had been when from upstairs she heard that shot—the shot that for a second had checked her breathing as if she herself had been hit. As clearly as if she had been in the room, she had seen Monte stretched out on the floor, with Hamilton bending over him. She had not thought of any other possibility. As she sprang down the stairs she had been sure of what she was about to see. But when she entered she had found Monte standing erect—erect and smiling, with his light hair all awry like a schoolboy's.

Then, sinking into the chair near the window,—this very chair beside which she now stood,—he had asked her to go out and attend to madame.

Come to think of it, it was odd that he had been smiling. It was not quite natural for one to smile over as serious a matter as that. After all, even if Teddy was melodramatic, even if his shot had missed its mark, it was not a matter to take lightly.

She seated herself in the chair he had occupied, and her hands dropped wearily to her side. Her fingers touched something sticky—something on the side of the chair next to the wall—something that the gendarmes had not noticed. She did not dare to move them. She was paralyzed, as if her fingers had met some cold, strange hand. For one second, two seconds, three seconds, she sat there transfixed, fearing, if she moved as much as a muscle, that something would spring at her from below—some awful fact.

Then finally she did move. She moved slowly, with her eyes closed. Then, suddenly opening them wide, she saw her fingers stained carmine. She knew then why Monte had smiled. It was like him to do that. Running swiftly to her room, she called Marie as she ran.

"Marie—my hat! Your hat! Hurry!"

"Oh, mon Dieu!" exclaimed Marie. "Has anything happened?"

"I have just learned what has already happened," she answered. "But do not alarm madame."

It was impossible not to alarm madame.

The mere fact that they were going out alarmed madame. Marjory stopped in the hall and quite coolly worked on her gloves.

"We are going for a little walk in the sunshine," she said. "Will you not come with us?"

Decidedly madame would not. She was too weak and faint. She should send for a friend to stay with her while she rested on her bed.

"That is best for you," nodded Marjory. "Au revoir."

With Marie by her side, she took her little walk in the sunshine, without hurrying, as far as around the first corner. Then she signaled for a cab, and showed the driver a louis d'or.

"Hôtel Normandie. This is for you—if you make speed," she said.

It was a wonder the driver was not arrested within a block; but it was nothing less than a miracle that he reached the hotel without loss of life. A louis d'or is a great deal of money, but these Americans are all mad. When Marie followed her mistress from the cab, she made a little prayer of thanks to the bon Dieu who had saved her life.

Mademoiselle inquired of the clerk for Monsieur Covington.

Yes, Monsieur Covington had reached the hotel some fifteen minutes before. But he was ill. He had met with an accident. Already a surgeon was with him.

"He—he is not badly injured?" inquired Marjory.

"I do not know," answered the clerk. "He was carried to his room in a faint. He was very white."

"I will wait in the writing-room. When the surgeon comes down I wish to see him. At once—do you understand?"

"Yes, mademoiselle."

Marie suspected what had happened. Monsieur Covington, too, had presented the driver with a louis d'or, and—miracles do not occur twice in one day.

Marjory seated herself by a desk, where she had a full view of the office—of all who came in and all who went out. That she was here doing this and that Monte Covington was upstairs wounded by a pistol shot was confusing, considering the fact that as short a time ago as yesterday evening she had not been conscious of the existence in Paris of either this hotel or of Monsieur Covington. Of the man who, on the other hand, had been disturbing her a great deal—this Teddy Hamilton—she thought not at all. It was as if he had ceased to exist. She did not even associate him, at this moment, with her presence here. She was here solely because of Monte.

He had stood by the window in Madame Courcy's dingy reception room, smiling—his hair all awry. She recalled many other details now: how his arm had hung limp; how he had been to a good deal of awkward trouble to keep his left arm always toward her; how white he had been when he passed her on his way out; how he had seemed to stumble when he stepped into the cab.

She must have been a fool not to understand that something was wrong with him—the more so because only a few minutes before that he had stood before her with his cheeks a deep red, his body firm, his eyes clear and bright.

That was when he had asked her to marry him. Monte Covington had asked her to marry him, and she had consented. With her chin in her hand, she thought that over. He had asked her in order that it might be his privilege to go downstairs and rid her of Teddy. It had been suggested in a moment, and she had consented in a moment. So, technically, she was at this moment engaged. The man upstairs was her fiancé. That gave her the right to be here. It was as if this had all been arranged beforehand to this very end.

It was this feature of her strange position that interested her. She had been more startled, more excited, when Monte proposed, than she was at this moment. It had taken away her breath at first; but now she was able to look at it quite coolly. He did not love her, he said. Good old Monte—honest and four-square. Of course he did not love her. Why should he? He was leading his life, with all the wide world to wander over, free to do this or to do that; utterly without care; utterly without responsibility.

It was this that had always appealed to her in him ever since she had first known him. It was this that had made her envious of him. It was exactly as she would have done in his circumstances. It was exactly as she tried to do when her own circumstances changed so that it had seemed possible. She had failed merely because she was a woman—because men refused to leave her free.

His proposal was merely that she share his freedom. Good old Monte—honest and four-square!

In return, there were little ways in which she might help him, even as he might help her; but they had come faster than either had expected.

Where was the surgeon? She rose and went to the clerk.

"Are you sure the surgeon has not gone?" she asked.

"Very sure," answered the clerk. "He has just sent out for a nurse to remain with monsieur."

"A nurse?" repeated Marjory.

"The doctor says Monsieur Covington must not be left alone."

"It's as bad—as that?" questioned Marjory.

"I do not know."

"I must see the doctor at once," she said. "But, first,—can you give me apartments on the same floor,—for myself and maid? I am his fiancée," she informed him.

"I can give mademoiselle apartments adjoining," said the clerk eagerly.

"Then do so."

She signed her name in the register, and beckoned for Marie.

"Marie," she said, "you may return and finish packing my trunks. Please bring them here."

"Here?" queried Marie.

"Here," answered Marjory.

She turned to the clerk.

"Take me upstairs at once."

There was a strong smell of ether in the hall outside the door of Monte Covington's room. It made her gasp for a moment. It seemed to make concrete what, after all, had until this moment been more or less vague. It was like fiction suddenly made true. That pungent odor was a grim reality. So was that black-bearded Dr. Marcellin, who, leaving his patient in the hands of his assistant, came to the door wiping his hands upon a towel.

"I am Mr. Covington's fiancée—Miss Stockton," she said at once. "You will tell me the truth?"

After one glance at her eyes Dr. Marcellin was willing to tell the truth.

"It is an ugly bullet wound in his shoulder," he said.

"It is not serious?"

"Such things are always serious. Luckily, I was able to find the bullet and remove it. It was a narrow escape for him."

"Of course," she added, "I shall serve as his nurse."

"Good," he nodded.

But he added, having had some experience with fiancées as nurses:—

"Of course I shall have for a week my own nurse also; but I shall be glad of your assistance. This—er—was an accident?"

She nodded.

"He was trying to save a foolish friend from killing himself."

"I understand."

"Nothing more need be said about it?"

"Nothing more," Dr. Marcellin assured her. "If you will come in I will give you your instructions. Mademoiselle Duval will soon be here."

"Is she necessary?" inquired Marjory. "I have engaged the next apartment for myself and maid."

"That is very good, but—Mademoiselle Duval is necessary for the present. Will you come in?"

She followed the doctor into Monsieur Covington's room. There the odor of ether hung still heavier.

She heard him muttering a name. She listened to catch it.

"Edhart," he called. "Oh, Edhart!"

CHAPTER VII
THE ADVANTAGES OF BEING SHOT

Under proper conditions, being wounded in the shoulder may have its pleasant features. They were not so obvious to Monte in the early part of the evening, because he was pretty much befuddled with ether; but sometime before dawn he woke up feeling fairly normal and clear-headed and interested. This was where fifteen years of clean living counted for something. When Marcellin and his assistant had first stripped Monte to the waist the day before, they had paused for a moment to admire what they called his torso. It was not often, in their city practice, that they ran across a man of thirty with muscles as clearly outlined as in an anatomical illustration.

Monte was conscious of a burning pain in his shoulder, and he was not quite certain as to where he was. So he hitched up on one elbow. This caused a shadow to detach itself from the dark at the other end of the room—a shadow that rustled and came toward him. It is small wonder that he was startled.

"Who the deuce are you?" he inquired in plain English.

"Monsieur is not to sit up," the shadow answered in plain French.

Monte repeated his question, this time in French.

"I am the nurse sent here by Dr. Marcellin," she informed him. "Monsieur is not to talk."

She placed her hand below his neck and helped him to settle down again upon his pillow. Then she rustled off again beyond the range of the shaded electric light.

"What happened?" Monte called into the dark.

Then he thought he heard a door open, and further rustling, and a whispered conversation.

"Who's that?" he demanded.

It sounded like a conspiracy of some sort, so he tried again to make his elbow. Mademoiselle appeared promptly, and, again placing her hand beneath his neck, lowered him once more to his pillow.

"Turn up the light, will you?" requested Monte.

"But certainly not," answered the nurse. "Monsieur is to lie very quiet and sleep."

"I can't sleep."

"Perhaps it will help monsieur to be quiet if he knows his fiancée is in the next room."

Momentarily this announcement appeared to have directly the opposite effect.

"My what?" gasped Monte.

"Monsieur's fiancée. With her maid, she is occupying the next apartment in order to be near monsieur. If you are very quiet to-night, it is possible that to-morrow the doctor will permit you to see her."

"Was that she who came in and whispered to you?"

"Yes, monsieur."

Monte remained quiet after that—but he was not sleeping. He was thinking.

In the first place, this was enough to make him recall all that had happened. This led him to speculate on all that might be about to happen—how much he could not at that moment even imagine. Neither line of thought was conducive to sleep.

Marjory was in the next room, awake, and at the sound of his voice had come in. In the dark, even with this great night city of Paris asleep around him, she had come near enough so that he heard the rustle of her skirt and her whispering voice. That was unusual—most unusual—and rather satisfactory. If worse came to worse and he reached a point where it was necessary for him to talk to some one, he could get her in here again in spite of this nurse woman. He had only to call her name. Not that he really had any intention in the world of doing it. The idea rather embarrassed him. He would not know what to say to a young lady at this hour of the night—even Marjory. But there she was—some one from home, some one he knew and who knew him. It was like having Edhart within reach.

In this last week he had sometimes awakened as he was now awake, and the silence had oppressed him. Ordinarily there was nothing morbid about Monte, but Edhart's death and the big empty space that was left all about Nice, the silence where once he had been sure of hearing Edhart's voice, the ghostly reminders of Edhart in those who clicked about in Edhart's bones without his flesh—all these things had given Monte's thoughts an occasional novel trend.

Once or twice he had gone as far as to picture himself as upon the point of death here in this foreign city. It was a very sad, a melancholy thing to speak about. He might call until he was hoarse, and no one would answer except possibly the night clerk or a gendarme. And they would look upon him only as something of a nuisance. It is really pathetic—the depths of misery into which a healthy man may, in such a mood, plunge himself.

All around him the dark, silent city, asleep save for the night clerks, the gendarmes, the evildoers, and the merrymakers. And these last would only leer at him. If he did not join them, then it was his fault if he lay dying alone.

"Is she in there now?" Monte called to the nurse in the dark.

"Certainly, monsieur. But I thought you were sleeping."

No, he was not sleeping; but he did not mind now the pain in his shoulder. She had announced herself as his fiancée. Well, technically, she was. He had asked her to marry him, and she had accepted. At the time he had not seen much farther ahead than the next few minutes; and even then had not foreseen what was to happen in those few minutes. The proposal had given him his right to talk to Hamilton, and her acceptance—well, it had given Marjory her right to be here.

Curious thing about that code of rights and wrongs! Society was a stickler for form. If either he or Marjory had neglected the preliminaries, then he might have lain here alone for a week, with society shaking its Puritan head. This nurse woman might have come, but she did not count; and, besides, he had to get shot before even she would be allowed.

Now it was all right. It was all right and proper for her, all right and proper for him, all right and proper for society. Not only that, but it was so utterly normal that society would have frowned if she had not hurried to his side in such an emergency. It forced her here, willy-nilly. Perhaps that was the only reason she was here.

Still, he did not like to think that. She was too true blue to quit a friend. It would be more like her to come anyway. He remembered how she had stood by that old aunt to the end. She would be standing by her to-day were she alive. Even Chic, who fulfilled his own obligations to the last word, had sometimes urged her to lead her own life, and she had only smiled. There was man stuff in her.

It showed when she announced to these people her engagement. He did not believe she did that either because it was necessary or proper. She did it because it was the literal truth, and she was not ashamed of the literal truth in anything.

"Is Mademoiselle Stockton sitting up—there in the next room?"

"I do not know," answered the nurse.

"Do you mind finding out for me?"

"If monsieur will promise to sleep after that."

"How can a man promise to sleep?"

Even under normal conditions, that was a foolish thing to promise. But when a man was experiencing brand-new sensations—the sensations of being engaged—it was quite impossible to make such a promise.

"Monsieur can at least promise not to talk."

"I will do that," agreed Monte.

She came back and reported that mademoiselle was sitting up, and begged to present her regards and express the hope that he was resting comfortably.

"Please to tell her I am, and that I hope she will now go to bed," he answered.

Nurse Duval did that, and returned.

"What did she say?" inquired Monte.

"But, monsieur—"

She had no intention of spending the rest of the night as a messenger between those two rooms.

"Very well," submitted Monte. "But you might tell me what she said."

"She said she was not sleepy," answered the nurse.

"I'm glad she's awake," said Monte.

Just because he was awake. In a sense, it gave them this city for themselves. It was as if this immediately became their city. That was not good arithmetic. Assuming that the city contained a population of three millions,—he did not have his Baedeker at hand,—then clearly he could consider only one three millionth part of the city as his. With her awake in the next room, that made only two of them, so that taken collectively they had a right to claim only two three-millionths parts as belonging to them. Yet that was not the way it worked out. As far as he was concerned, the other two millions nine hundred and ninety-nine thousand nine hundred and ninety-eight did not exist.

There was nothing sentimental about this conclusion. He did not think of it as it affected her—merely as it affected him. It gave him rather a comfortable, completed feeling, as if he now had within himself the means for peacefully enjoying life, wherever he might be, even at thirty-two. Under the influence of this soothing thought, he fell asleep again.

After the doctors were through with Monte the next morning, they decided, after a consultation, that there was no apparent reason why, during the day,

Miss Stockton, if she desired, should not serve as his nurse while Miss Duval went home to sleep.

"My assistant will come in at least twice," said Dr. Marcellin. "Besides, you have the constitution of a prize-fighter. It might well be possible to place a bullet through the heart of such a man without greatly discommoding him."

He spoke as if with some resentment.

After they had gone out, Marjory came in. She hesitated at the door a moment, perhaps to make sure that he was awake; perhaps to make sure that she herself was awake. Monte, from the bed, could see her better than she could see him. He thought she looked whiter than usual, but she was very beautiful.

There was something about her that distinguished her from other women—from this nurse woman, for example, who was the only other woman with whom it was possible to compare her in a like situation. With one hand resting on the door, her chin well up, she looked more than ever like Her Royal Highness Something or Other. She was dressed in something white and light and fluffy, like the gowns he used to see on Class Day. Around her white throat there was a narrow band of black velvet.

"Good-morning, Marjory," he called.

She came at once to his side, walking graciously, as a princess might walk.

"I did n't know if you were awake," she said.

It was one thing to have her here in the dark, and another to have her here in broad daylight. The sun was streaming in at the windows now, and outside the birds were chattering.

"Did you rest well last night?" she inquired.

"I heard you when you came in and whispered to the nurse woman. It was mighty white of you to come."

"What else could I do?" She seated herself in a chair by his bed.

"Because we are engaged?" he asked.

She smiled a little as he said that.

"Then you have not forgotten?"

"Forgotten!" he exclaimed. "I'm just beginning to realize it."

"I was afraid it might come back to you as a shock, Monte," she said. "But it is very convenient—at just this time."

"I don't know what I should have done without it," he nodded. "It certainly gives a man a comfortable feeling to know—well, just to know there is some one around."

"I'm glad if I've been able to do anything."

"It's a whole lot just having you here," he assured her.

It changed the whole character of this room, for one thing. It ceased to be merely a hotel room—merely number fifty-four attached with a big brass star to a key. It was more like a room in the Hôtel des Roses, which was the nearest to home of any place Monte had found in a decade. It was as if when she came in she completely refurnished it with little things with which he was familiar. Edhart always used to place flowers in his apartment; and it was like that.

"The only bother with the arrangement," he said, looking serious, "is that it takes your time. Ought n't you to be at Julien's this morning?"

She had forgotten about Julien's. Yet for the last two years it had been the very center of her own individual life. Now the crowded studio, the smell of turpentine, the odd cosmopolitan gathering of fellow students, the little pangs following the bitter criticisms of the master, receded into the background until they became as a dream of long ago.

"I don't think I shall ever go to Julien's again," she answered.

"But look here—that won't do," he objected. "If I'm to interfere with all your plans—"

"It isn't that, Monte," she assured him. "Ever since I came back this last time, I knew I did n't belong there. When Aunt Kitty was alive it was all the opportunity I had; but now—" She paused.

"Well?"

"I have my hands full with you until you get out again," she answered lightly.

"That's what I object to," he said; "If being engaged is going to pin you down, then I don't think you ought to be engaged. You've had enough of that in your life."

The curious feature of her present position was that she had no sense of being pinned down. She had thought of this in the night. She had never felt freer in her life. Within a few hours of her engagement she had been able to do exactly what she wished to do without a single qualm of conscience. She had been able to come here and look after him in this emergency. She would have done this anyway, but she knew how Marcellin and his assistant and even Nurse Duval would have made her pay for her act—an act based upon nothing but decent loyalty and honest responsibility. Raised eyebrows—gossip in the air—covert smiles—the whole detestable atmosphere of intrigue with which they would have surrounded her, had vanished as by a spell before the magic word fiancée. She was breathing air like that upon the mountain-tops. It was sweet and clean and bracing.

"Monte," she said, "I'm doing at this moment just exactly what I want to do; and you can't understand what a treat that is, because you've always done just exactly as you wanted. I 'm sure I 'm entirely selfish about this, because—because I'm not making any sacrifice. You can't understand that, either, Monte,—so please don't try. I think we'd better not talk any more about it. Can't we just let it go on as it is a little while?"

"It suits me," smiled Monte. "So maybe I'm selfish, too."

"Maybe," she nodded. "Now I'll see about your breakfast. The doctor told me just what you must have."

So she went out—moving away like a vision in dainty white across the room and out the door. A few minutes later she was back again with a vase of red roses, which she arranged upon the table where he could see them.

CHAPTER VIII
DRAWBACKS OF RECOVERY

Monte's recovery was rapid—in many ways more rapid than he desired. In a few days Nurse Duval disappeared, and in a few days more Monte was able to dress himself with the help of the hotel valet, and sit by the window while Marjory read to him. Half the time he gave no heed to what she was reading, but that did not detract from his pleasure in the slightest. He liked the sound of her voice, and liked the idea of sitting opposite her.

Her eyes were always interesting when she read. For then she forgot about them and let them have their own way—now to light with a smile, now to darken with disapproval, and sometimes to grow very tender, as the story she happened to be reading dictated.

This was luxury such as Monte had never known, and for more than ten years now he had ordered of the world its choicest in the way of luxury.

At his New York club the experience of many, many years in catering to man comfort was placed at his disposal. As far as possible, every desire was anticipated, so that little more effort was required of him than merely to furnish the desires. In a house where no limit whatever had been set upon the expense, a hundred lackeys stood ready to jump if a man as much as raised an eyebrow. And they understood, those fellows, what a man needs—from the chef who searched the markets of the world to satisfy tender tastes, to the doorman who acquainted himself with the names of the members and their personal idiosyncrasies.

That same service was furnished him, if to a more limited extent, on the transatlantic liners, where Monte's name upon the passenger list was immediately passed down the line with the word that he must have the best. At Davos his needs were anticipated a week in advance; at Nice there had been Edhart, who added his smiling self to everything else.

But no one at his club, on the boat, or at Davos—not even Edhart—had given him this: this being the somewhat vague word he used to describe what he was now enjoying as Marjory sat by the window reading to him. It had nothing to do with being read aloud to. He could at any time have summoned a valet to do that, and in five minutes would have felt like throwing the book—any book—at the valet's head. It had nothing to do with the mere fact that she was a woman. Nurse Duval could not have taken her place. Kind as she had been, he was heartily bored with her before she left.

It would seem, then, that in some mysterious way he derived his pleasure from Marjory herself. But, if so, then she had gone farther than all those who made it their life-work to see that man was comfortable; for they satisfied only existing wants, while she created a new one. Whenever she left the room he was conscious of this want.

Yet, when Monte faced the issue squarely and asked himself if this were not a symptom of being in love, he answered it as fairly as he could out of an experience that covered Chic Warren's pre-nuptial brain-storms; a close observation of several dozen honeymoon couples on shipboard, to say nothing of many incipient cases which started there; and, finally, the case of Teddy Hamilton.

The leading feature of all those distressing examples seemed to indicate that, while theoretically the man was in an ideal state of blissful ecstasy, he was, practically, in a condition bordering on madness. At the very moment he was supposed to be happy, he was about half the time most miserable. Even at its best, it did not make for comfort. Poor Chic ran the gamut every week from hell to heaven. It was with a sigh of relief that Monte was able to answer his own question conscientiously in the negative. It was just because he was able to retain the use of his faculties that he was able to enjoy the situation.

Monte liked to consider himself thoroughly normal in everything. As far as he had any theory of life, it was based upon the wisdom of keeping cool—of keeping normal. To get the utmost out of every day, this was necessary. It was not the man who drank too much who enjoyed his wine: it was the man who drank little. That was true of everything. If Hamilton had only kept his head—well, after all, Monte was indebted to Hamilton for not having kept his head.

Monte was not in love: that was certain. Marjory was not in love: that also was certain. This was why he was able to light his cigarette, lean back his head on the pillow she arranged, and drift into a state of dreamy content as she read to him. This happy arrangement might go on forever except that, in the course of time, his shoulder was bound to heal. And then—he knew well enough that old Dame Society was even at the end of these first ten days beginning to fidget. He knew that Marjory knew it, too. It began the day Dr. Marcellin advised him to take a walk in the Champs Élysées.

He was perfectly willing to do that. It was beautiful out there. They sat down at one of the little iron tables—the little tables were so warm and sociable now—and beneath the whispering trees sipped their café au lait. But the fact that he was able to get out of his room seemed to make a difference in their thoughts. It was as if his status had changed. It was as if those who passed him, with a glance at his arm in its sling, stopped to tell him so.

It was none of their business, at that. It would have been sheer presumption of them to have butted into any of the other affairs of his life: whether he was losing money or making money; whether he was going to England or to

Spain, or going to remain where he was; whether he preferred chops for breakfast, or bread and coffee. Theoretically, then, it was sheer presumption for them to interest themselves in the question of whether he was an invalid confined to his room, or a convalescent able to get out, or a man wholly recovered.

Yet he knew that, with every passing day that he came out into the sunshine, these same people were managing to make Marjory's position more and more delicate. It became increasingly less comfortable for her and for him when they returned to the hotel.

Therefore he was not greatly surprised when she remarked one morning:—

"Monte, I've been thinking over where I shall go, and I 've about decided to go to Étois."

"When?" he asked.

"Very soon—before the end of the week, anyway."

"But look here!" he protested. "What am I going to do?"

"I don't know," she smiled. "But one thing is certain: you can't play sick very much longer."

"The doctor says it will be another two weeks before my arm is out of the sling."

"Even so, the rest of you is well. There is n't much excuse for my bringing in your breakfasts, Monte."

"Do you mind doing it?"

"No."

"Who is to tie on this silk handkerchief?" He wore a black silk handkerchief over his bandages, which she always adjusted for him.

She met his eyes a moment, and smiled again.

"I'm going to Étois," she said. "I think I shall get a little villa there and stay all summer."

"Then," he declared, "I think I shall go to Étois myself."

"I 'm afraid you must n't."

"But the doctor says I must n't play golf for six months. What do you think I'm going to do with myself until then?"

"There's all the rest of the world," she suggested.

Monte frowned.

"Are you going to break our engagement, then?"

"It has served its purpose, hasn't it?" she asked.

"Up to now," he admitted. "But you say it can't go any farther."

"No, Monte."

The next suggestion that leaped into Monte's mind was obvious enough, yet he paused a moment before voicing it. Perhaps even then he would not have found the courage had he not been rather panic-stricken. He had exactly the same feeling, when he thought of her in Étois, that he had when he thought of Edhart in Paradise. It started as resentment, but ended in a slate-gray loneliness.

He could imagine himself as sitting here alone at one of these little iron tables, and decidedly it was not pleasant. When he pictured himself as returning to his room in the hotel and to the company of the hotel valet, it put him in a mood that augured ill for the valet.

It would have been bad enough had he been able to resume his normal schedule and fill his time with golf; but, with even that relaxation denied him, such a situation as she proposed was impossible. For the present, at any rate, she was absolutely indispensable. She ought to know that a valet could not adjust a silk handkerchief properly, and that without this he could not even go upon the street. And who would read to him from the American papers?

There was no further excuse, she said, for her to bring in his breakfasts, but if she did not sit opposite him at breakfast, what in thunder was the use of eating breakfast? If she had not begun breakfasting with him, then he would never have known the difference. But she had begun it; she had first suggested it. And now she calmly proposed turning him over to a valet.

"Marjory," he said, "didn't I ask you to marry me?"

She nodded.

"That was necessary in order that we might be engaged," she reminded him.

"Exactly," he agreed. "Now there seems to be only one way that we may keep right on being engaged."

"I don't see that, Monte," she answered. "We may keep on being engaged as long as we please, may n't we?"

"It seems not. That is, there is n't much sense in it if it won't let me go to Étois with you."

"Of course you can't do that."

"And yet," he said, "if we were married I could go, couldn't I?"

"Why—er—yes," she faltered; "I suppose so."

"Then," he said, "why don't we get married?"

She did not turn away her head. She lifted her dark eyes to his.

"Just what do you mean, Monte?" she demanded.

"I mean," he said uneasily, "that we should get married just so that we can go on—as we have been these last ten days. Really, we'll still only be engaged, but no one need know that. Besides, no one will care, if we're married."

He gained confidence as he went on, though he was somewhat afraid of the wonder in her eyes.

"People don't care anything more about you after you're married," he said. "They just let you drop as if you were done for. It's a queer thing, but they do. Why, if we were married we could sit here all day and no one would give us a second glance. We could have breakfast together as often as we wished, and no one would care a hang. I've seen it done. We could go to Étois together, and I could pay for half the villa and you could pay for half. You can bring Marie, and we can stay as long as we wish without having any one turn an eye."

He was growing enthusiastic now.

"There will be nothing to prevent you from doing just as you wish. You can paint all day if you want. You can paint yards of things—olive trees and sky and rocks. There are lots of them around Étois. And I—"

"Yes," she interrupted; "what can you do, Monte?"

"I can watch you paint," he answered. "Or I can walk. Or I can—oh, there'll be plenty for me to do. If we tire of Étois we can move somewhere else. If we tire of each other's company, why, we can each go somewhere else. It's simple, is n't it? We can both do just as we please, can't we? There won't be a living soul with the right to open his head to us. Do you get that? Why, even if you want to go off by yourself, with Mrs. in front of your name they'll let you alone."

At first she had been surprised, then she had been amused, but now she was thinking.

"It's queer, is n't it, Monte, that it should be like that?"

"It's the way it is. It makes everything simple and puts the whole matter up to us."

"Yes," she admitted thoughtfully.

"Of course," he said, "I'm assuming you don't mind having me around quite a lot."

"No, I don't mind that," she assured him. "But I'm wondering if you'll mind—having me around?"

"I did n't realize until this last week how—well, how comfortable it was having you around," he confessed.

She glanced up.

"Yes," she said, "that's the word. I think we've made each other comfortable. After all—that's something."

"It's a whole lot."

"And it need n't ever be anything else, need it?"

"Certainly not," he declared. "That would spoil everything. That's what we're trying to avoid."

To his surprise, she suddenly rose as if to leave.

"Look here!" he exclaimed. "Can't we settle this right now—so that we won't have to worry about it?"

He disliked having anything left to worry about.

"I should think the least you'd expect of me would be to think it over," she answered.

"It would be so much simpler just to go ahead," he declared.

There seemed to be no apparent reason in the world why she should not assent to Monte's proposal. In and of itself, the arrangement offered her exactly what she craved—the widest possible freedom to lead her own life without let or hindrance from any one, combined with the least possible responsibility. As far as she could see, it would remove once and for all the single fretting annoyance that, so far, had disarranged all her plans.

Monte's argument was sound. Once she was married, the world of men would let her alone. So, too, would the world of women. She could face them both with a challenge to dispute her privileges. All this she would receive without any of the obligations with which most women pay so heavily for their release from the bondage in which they are held until married. For they pay even more when they love—pay the more, in a way, the more they love. It cannot be helped.

She was thinking of the Warrens—the same Warrens Monte had visited when Chic, Junior had the whooping cough. She had been there when Chic, Junior was born. Marion had wanted her near—in the next room. She had learned then how they pay—these women who love.

She had been there at other times—less dramatic times. It was just the same. From the moment Marion awoke in the morning until she sank wearily into her bed at night, her time, her thought, her heart, her soul almost, was claimed by some one else. She gave, gave, until nothing was left for herself.

Marjory, in her lesser way, had done much the same—so she knew the cost. It was rare when she had been able to leave her aunt for a whole day and night. Year after year, she too had awakened in the morning to her tasks for another—for this woman who had demanded them as her right. She too had given her time, her thought, her soul, almost, to another. If she had not given her heart, it was perhaps because it was not asked; perhaps, again, it was because she had no heart to give.

Sometimes, in that strange, emotionless existence she had lived so long where duty took the place of love, she had wondered about that. If she had a heart, it never beat any faster to let her know she had it.

She paid her debt of duty in full—paid until her release came. In the final two weeks of her aunt's life she had never left her side. Patiently, steadfastly, she helped with all there was in her to fight that last fight. When it was over, she did not break down, as the doctors predicted. She went to bed and slept forty-eight hours, and awoke ten years younger.

She awoke as one out of bondage, and stared with keen, eager eyes at a new world. For a few weeks she had twenty-four hours a day of her own. Then Peter had come, and others had come, and finally Teddy had come. They wanted to take from her that which she had just gained—each in his own fashion.

"Give us of yourself," they pleaded. "Begin again your sacrifices."

Peter put it best, even though he did not say much. But she had only to look in his eyes and read his proposal.

"Come with me and stand by my side while I carve my career," was what his eyes said. "I'll love you and make you love me as Marion loves. You'll begin the day with me, and you'll guard my home while I'm gone until night, and you'll share my honors and my disappointments, and perhaps a time will come when Marion will stand in the next room, as once you stood in the next room. Then—"

It was at this point she drew back. Then her soul would go out into the newborn soul, and after that she would only live and breathe and hope through that other. When Marion laughed and said that she was as she was because she did not know, Marion was wrong. It was because she did know—because she knew how madly and irrevocably she would give, if ever she gave again. There would be nothing left for herself at all. It would be as if she had died.

She did not wish to give like that. She wished to live a little. She wished to be herself a little—herself as she now was. She wished to get back some of those years between seventeen and twenty-seven—taste the world as it was then.

What Teddy offered was different. Something was there that even Peter did not have—something that made her catch her breath once or twice when he sang to her like a white-robed choir-boy. It was as if he asked her to take his hand and jump with him into a white-hot flame. He carried her farther back in her passions than Peter did—back to seventeen, back to the primitive, elemental part of her. He really made her heart beat. But on guard within her stood the older woman, and she could not move.

Now came Monte—asking nothing. He asked nothing because he wished to give nothing. She was under no illusion about that. There was not anything idealistic about Monte. This was to be purely an arrangement for their mutual comfort. They were to be companions on an indefinite tour of the world—each paying his own bills.

At thirty-two he needed a comrade of some sort, and in his turn he offered himself as an escort. She found no apparent reason, then, even when she had spent half the night getting as far as this, why she should not immediately accept his proposal. Yet she still hesitated.

It was not that she did not trust Monte. Not the slightest doubt in the world existed in her mind about that. She would trust him farther than she would even Peter—trust him farther than any man she had ever met. He was four-square, and she knew it. Perhaps it was a curious suggestion—it was just because of this that she hesitated.

In a way, she was considering Monte. She did not like to help him give up responsibilities that might be good for him. She was somewhat disappointed that he was willing to give them up. He did not have the excuse she had—years of self-sacrifice. He had been free all his life to indulge himself, and he had done so. He had never known a care, never known a heartache. Having money, he had used it decently, so that he had avoided even the compensating curse that is supposed to come with money.

She knew there was a lot to Monte. She had sensed that from the first. He had proved it in the last two weeks. It only needed some one to bring it out, and he would average high. Love might do it—the same white-hot love that had driven Teddy mad.

But that was what he was avoiding, just as she was. Well, what of it? If one did not reach the heights, then one did not sound the depths. After all, it was not within her province to direct Monte's life. She was selfish—she had warned him of that. He was selfish—and had warned her.

Yet, as she lay there in her bed, she felt that she was about to give up something forever, and that Monte was about to give up something forever. It is one thing not to want something, and another to make an irrevocable decision never to have it. Also, it is one thing to fret one's self into an unnecessary panic over a problem at night, and another to handle it lightly in the balmy sunshine of a Parisian springtime morning.

Monte had risen early and gone out and bought her violets again. When she came in, he handed them to her, and she buried her face in their dewy fragrance. It was good to have some one think of just such little attentions. Then, too, his boyish enthusiasm swept her off her guard. He was so eager and light-hearted this morning that she found herself breaking into a laugh. She was still laughing when he brought back to her last night's discussion.

"Well, have you decided to marry me?" he demanded.

She shook her head, her face still buried in the violets.

"What's worrying you about it?" he asked.

"You, Monte," she answered.

"I? Well, that isn't much. I looked up the time-tables, and we could take the six-ten to-night if you were ready."

"I could n't possibly be ready," she replied decidedly.

"To-morrow, then?"

When he insisted upon being definite, the proposition sounded a great deal more absurd than when he allowed it to be indefinite. She was still hesitating when Marie appeared.

"A telephone for mademoiselle," she announced.

Monte heard her startled exclamation from the next room. He hurried to the door. She saw him, and, placing her hand over the telephone, turned excitedly.

"It's Teddy again," she trembled.

"Let me talk to him," he commanded.

"He says he does n't believe in our—our engagement."

"We're to be married to-morrow?" he asked quickly.

"We're to be married to-morrow?"

"Oh!"

"It's the only way to get rid of him."

"Then—"

"To-morrow?"

Catching her breath, she nodded.

He took the receiver.

"This is Covington," he said. "Miss Stockton and I are to be married to-morrow. Get that?... Well, keep hold of it, because the moment I 'm her husband—"

Following an oath at the other end, Monte heard the click of the receiver as it was snapped up.

"That settles it very nicely," he smiled.

CHAPTER IX
BLUE AND GOLD

Marjory was to be married on June eighteenth, at eleven o'clock, in the chapel of the English Congregational Church. At ten o'clock of that day she was in her room before the mirror, trying to account for her heightened color. Marie had just left her in despair and bewilderment, after trying to make her look as bridelike as possible when she did not wish to look bridelike. Marie had wished to do her hair in some absurd new fashion for the occasion.

"But, Marie," she had explained, "nothing is to be changed. Therefore why should I change my appearance?"

"Mademoiselle to be a bride—and nothing changed?" Marie had cried.

"Nothing about me; nothing about Mr. Covington. We are merely to be married, that is all—as a matter of convenience."

"Mademoiselle will see," Marie had answered cryptically.

"You will see yourself," Marjory had laughed.

Eh bien! something was changed already, as she had only to look in the mirror to observe. There was a deep flush upon her cheeks and her eyes did not look quite natural. She saw, and seeing only made it worse. Manifestly it was absurd of her to become excited now over a matter that up to this point she had been able to handle so reasonably. It was scarcely loyal to Monte. He had a right to expect her to be more sensible.

He had put it well last night when he had remarked that for her to go to a chapel to be married was no more serious than to go to an embassy for a passport. She was merely to share with him the freedom that was his as a birthright of his sex. In no other respect whatever was she to be under any obligations to him. With ample means of her own, he was simply giving her an opportunity to enjoy them unmolested—a privilege which the world denied her as long as she remained unmarried. In no way was he to be responsible for her or to her. He understood this fully, and it was exactly what he himself desired.

She, in return for this privilege, was to make herself as entertaining a traveling companion as possible. She was to be what she had been these last few weeks.

Neither was making any sacrifice. That was precisely what they were avoiding. That was the beauty of the arrangement. Instead of multiplying cares and responsibilities, as ordinary folk did,—thereby defeating the very object for which they married, a fuller and wider freedom,—each was to do away with the few they already had as individuals.

Therefore it seemed scarcely decent for Marie to speak of her as a bride. Perhaps that accounted for the color. No sentiment was involved here. This was what made the arrangement possible. Sentiment involved caring; and, as Monte had once said, "It's the caring that seems to make the trouble." That was the trouble with the Warrens. How she cared—from morning till night, with her whole heart and soul in a flutter—for Chic and the children. In a different way, Marjory supposed, Teddy cared. This was the one thing that made him so impossible. In another way, Peter Noyes cared.

She gave a quick start as she thought of Peter Noyes. She turned away from the mirror as if—as if ashamed. She sprang to her feet, with an odd, tense expression about her mouth. It was as if she were looking into his dark, earnest eyes. Peter had always been so intensely in earnest about everything. In college he had worked himself thin to lead his class. In the law school he had graduated among the first five, though he came out almost half blind. His record, however, had won for him a place with a leading law firm in New York, where in his earnest way he was already making himself felt. It was just this quality that had frightened her. He had made love to her with his lips set as if love were some great responsibility. He had talked of duty and the joy of sacrifice until she had run away from him.

That had been her privilege. That had been her right. She had been under no obligation to him then; she was under no obligation to him now. Her life was hers, to do with as she saw fit. He had no business to intrude himself, at this of all times, upon her.

Not daring to look in the mirror again, she called Marie to adjust her hat and veil.

"It is half past ten, Marie," she announced nervously. "I—I think Monsieur Covington must be waiting for us."

"Yes, mademoiselle."

Her ears caught at the word.

"Marie."

"Yes, mademoiselle."

"I wish—even after this—to have you always address me as mademoiselle."

"But that—"

"It is my wish."

It was a blue-and-gold morning, with the city looking as if it had received a scrubbing during the night. So too did Monte, who was waiting below for her. Clean-shaven and ruddy, in a dark-gray morning coat and top hat, he looked very handsome, even with his crippled arm. And quite like a bridegroom! For a moment he made her wish she had taken Marie's advice about her hair. She was in a brown traveling suit with a piquant hat that made her look quite Parisienne—though her low tan shoes, tied with big silk bows at her trim ankles, were distinctly American.

Monte was smiling.

"You are n't afraid?" he asked.

"Of what, Monte?"

"I don't know. We 're on our way."

She took a long look at his steady blue eyes. They braced her like wine.

"You must never let me be afraid," she answered.

"Then—en avant!" he called.

In a way, it was a pity that they could not have been married out of doors. They should have gone into a garden for the ceremony instead of into the subdued light of the chapel. Then, too, it would have been much better had the Reverend Alexander Gordon been younger. He was a gentle, saintly-looking man of sixty, but serious—terribly serious. He had lived long in Paris, but instead of learning to be gay he had become like those sad-faced priests at Notre Dame. Perhaps if he had understood better the present circumstances he would have entered into the occasion instead of remaining so very solemn.

As Marjory shook hands with him she lost her bright color. Then, too, he had a voice that made her think again of Peter Noyes. In sudden terror she clung to Monte's arm, and during the brief ceremony gave her responses in a whisper.

Peter Noyes himself could not have made of this journey to the embassy a more trying ordeal. A ring was slipped upon the fourth finger of her left hand. A short prayer followed, and an earnest "God bless you, my children," which left her feeling suffocated. She thought Monte would never finish talking with him—would never get out into the sunshine again. When he did, she shrank away from the glare of the living day.

Monte gave a sigh of relief.

"That's over, anyhow," he said.

Hearing a queer noise behind him, he turned. There stood Marie, sniffling and wiping her eyes.

"Good Heavens," he demanded, "what's this?"

Marjory instantly moved to the girl's side.

"There—there," she soothed her gently; "it's only the excitement, n'est ce pas?"

"Yes, madame; and you know I wish you all happiness."

"And me also?" put in Monte.

"It goes without saying that monsieur will be happy."

He thrust some gold-pieces into her hand.

"Then drink to our good health with your friends," he suggested.

Calling a taxicab, he assisted her in; but before the door closed Marjory leaned toward her and whispered in her ear:—

"You will come back to the hotel at six?"

"Yes, madame."

So Marie went off to her cousins, looking in some ways more like a bride than her mistress.

Marjory preferred to walk. She wanted to get back again to the mood of half an hour ago. She must in some way get Peter Noyes out of her mind. So quite aimlessly they moved down the Avenue Montaigne, and Monte waved his hand at the passing people.

"Now," he announced, "you are none of anybody's business."

"Is that true, Monte?" Marjory asked eagerly.

"True as preaching."

"And no one has any right to scold me?"

"Not the slightest. If any one tries it, turn him over to me."

"That might not always be possible."

"You don't mean to say any one has begun this soon?"

He glared about as if to find the culprit.

"Don't look so fierce, Monte," she protested, with a laugh.

"Then don't you look so worried," he retorted.

Already, by his side, she was beginning to recover. A Parisian dandy coming toward them stared rather overlong at her. An hour ago it would have made her uneasy; now she felt like making a face at him.

She laughed a little.

"The minister was terribly serious, was n't he, Monte?"

"Too darned serious," he nodded. "But, you see, he did n't know. I suppose the cross-your-throat, hope-to-die kind of marriage is serious. That's the trouble with it."

"Yes; that's the trouble with it."

"I can see Chic coming down the aisle now, with his face chalk-white and—"

"Don't," she broke in.

He looked down at her—surprised that she herself was taking this so seriously.

"My comrade," he said, "what you need is to play a little."

"Yes," she agreed eagerly.

"Then where shall we go? The world is before you."

He was in exactly the mood to which she herself had looked forward—a mood of springtime and irresponsibility. That was what he should be. It was her right to feel like that also.

"Oh," she exclaimed, "I'd like to go to all the places I could n't go alone! Take me."

"To the Café de Paris for lunch?"

She nodded.

"To the races afterward and to the Riche for dinner?"

"Yes, yes."

"So to the theater and to Maxim's?"

Her face was flushed as she nodded again.

"We're off!" he exclaimed, taking her arm.

It was an afternoon that left her no time to think. She was caught up by the gay, care-free crowd and swept around in a dizzy circle. Yet always Monte was by her side. She could take his arm if she became too confused, and that always steadied her.

Then she was whirled back to the hotel and to Marie, with no more time than was necessary to dress for dinner. She was glad there was no more time. For at least to-day there must be no unfilled intervals. She felt refreshed after her bath, and, to Marie's delight, consented to attire herself in one of her newest evening gowns, a costume of silk and lace that revealed her neck and arms. Also she allowed Marie to do her hair as she pleased. That was a good sign, but Marie thought madame's cheeks did not look like a good sign.

"I hope madame—"

"Have you so soon forgotten what I asked of you?" Marjory interrupted.

"I hope mademoiselle," Marie corrected herself, "has not caught a fever."

"I should hope not," exclaimed Marjory. "What put that into your head?"

"Mademoiselle's cheeks are very hot."

Marjory brought her hand to her face. It did not feel hot, because her hands were equally hot.

"It is nothing but the excitement that brings the color," she informed Marie. "I have been living almost like a nun; and now—to get out all at once takes away one's breath.

"Also being a bride."

"Marie!"

"Eh bien, madame—mademoiselle was married only this morning."

"You do not seem to understand," Marjory explained; "but it is necessary that you should understand. Monsieur Covington is to me only like—like a big brother. It is in order that he might be with me as a big brother we went through the ceremony. People about here talk a great deal, and I have taken his name to prevent that. That is all. And you are to remain with me and everything is to go on exactly as before, he in his apartments and we in ours. You understand now?"

At least, Marie heard.

"It is rather an amusing situation, is it not?" demanded Marjory.

"I—I do not know," replied Marie.

"Then in time you shall see. In the mean while, you might smile. Why do you not smile?"

"I—I do not know," Marie replied honestly.

"You must learn how. It is necessary. It is necessary even to laugh. Monsieur Covington laughed a great deal this afternoon."

"He—he is a man," observed Marie, as if that were some explanation.

"Eh bien—is it men alone who have the privilege of laughing?"

"I do not know," answered Marie; "but I have noticed that men laugh a great deal more about some things than women."

"Then that is because women are fools," affirmed Marjory petulantly.

Though Marie was by no means convinced, she was ready to drop the matter in her admiration of the picture her mistress made when properly gowned. Whether she wished or not, madame, when she was done with her this evening, looked as a bride should look. And monsieur, waiting below, was worthy of her.

In his evening clothes he looked at least a foot taller than usual. Marie saw his eyes warm as he slipped over madame's beautiful white shoulders her evening wrap.

Monsieur's eyes warmed as he slipped the wrap over madame's shoulders

Before madame left she turned and whispered in Marie's ear.

"I may be late," she said; "but you will be here when I return."

"Yes, mademoiselle."

"Without fail?"

"Yes, mademoiselle."

Marie watched monsieur take his bride's arm as they went out the door, and the thing she whispered to herself had nothing to do with madame at all.

"Poor monsieur!" she said.

CHAPTER X
THE AFFAIR AT MAXIM'S

It was all new to Marjory. In the year and a half she had lived in Paris with her aunt she had dined mostly in her room. Such cafés as this she had seen only occasionally from a cab on her way to the opera. As she stood at the entrance to the big room, which sparkled like a diamond beneath a light, she was as dazed as a debutante entering her first ballroom. The head waiter, after one glance at Monte, was bent upon securing the best available table. Here was an American prince, if ever he had seen one.

Had monsieur any choice?

Decidedly. He desired a quiet table in a corner, not too near the music.

Such a table was immediately secured, and as Covington crossed the room with Marjory by his side he was conscious of being more observed than ever he had been when entering the Riche alone. His bandaged arm lent him a touch of distinction, to be sure; but this served only to turn eyes back again to Marjory, as if seeking in her the cause for it. She moved like a princess, with her head well up and her dark eyes brilliant.

"All eyes are upon you," he smiled, when he had given his order.

"If they are it's very absurd," she returned.

Also, if they were, it did not matter. That was the fact she most appreciated. Ever since she had been old enough to observe that men had eyes, it had been her duty to avoid those eyes. That had been especially true in Paris, and still more especially true in the few weeks she had been there alone.

Now, with Monte opposite her, she was at liberty to meet men's eyes and study them with interest. There was no danger. It was they who turned away from her—after a glance at Monte. It amused her to watch them turn away; it gave her a new sense of power. But of one thing she was certain: there was not a man in the lot with whom she would have felt comfortable to be here as she felt comfortable with Monte.

Monte was having a very pleasant time of it. The thing that surprised him was the way Marjory quickened his zest in old things that had become stale. Here, for instance, she took him back to the days when he had responded with a piquant tingle to the lights and the music and the gay Parisian chatter, to the quick glance of smiling eyes where adventure lurked. He had been content to observe without accepting the challenges, principally because he lived mostly in the sunshine. To-night, in a clean, decent way, he felt again the old tingle. But this time it came from a different source. When Marjory raised her eyes to his, the lights blazed as brilliantly as if a hundred new ones had been lighted; the music mixed with his blood until his thoughts danced.

With the coffee he lighted a cigarette and leaned back contentedly until it was time to go.

As they went out of the room, he was aware that once again all eyes were turned toward her, so that he threw back his shoulders a little farther than usual and looked about with some scorn at those who had with them only ordinary women.

The comedy at the Gymnase was sufficiently amusing to hold her attention, and that was the best she could ask for; but Monte watched it indifferently, resenting the fact that it did hold her attention. Besides, there were too many people all about her here. For two hours and a half it was as if she had gone back into the crowd. He was glad when the final curtain rang down and he was able to take her arm and guide her out.

"Maxim's next?" he inquired.

"Do you want to go?" she asked.

"It's for you to decide," he answered.

She was dead tired by now, but she did not dare to stop.

"All right," she said; "we'll go."

It was a harlequin crowd at Maxim's—a noisier, tenser, more hectic crowd than at the Riche. The room was gray with smoke, and everywhere she looked were gold-tipped wine bottles. Though it was still early, there was much hysterical laughter and much tossing about of long streamers of colored paper and confetti. As they entered she instinctively shrank away from it. Had the waiter delayed another second before leading them to a table, she would have gone out.

Monte ordered the wine he was expected to order, but Marjory scarcely touched it to her lips, while he was content to watch it bubble in his glass. He did not like to have her here, and yet it was almost worth the visit to watch her eyes grow big, to watch her sensitive mouth express the disgust she felt for the mad crowd, to have her unconsciously hitch her chair nearer his.

"The worst of it is," he explained to her, "it's the outsiders who are doing all this—Americans, most of them."

Suddenly, from behind them, a clear tenor voice made itself heard through the din. The first notes were indistinct; but in a few seconds the singer had the room to himself. Turning quickly, Marjory saw the slender figure of

Hamilton, swaying slightly, standing by a table, his eyes leveled upon hers. He was singing "The Rosary"—singing it as only he, when half mad, could sing it.

She clutched Monte's hand as he half rose from his seat.

"Please," she whispered, "it's best to sit still."

Stronger and stronger the plaintive melody fell from his lips, until finally the orchestra itself joined. Women strained forward, and half-dazed men sat back and listened with bated breath. Even Monte forgot for a moment the boldness that inspired Hamilton, and became conscious only of Marjory's warm fingers within his. So, had the singer been any one else, he would have been content to sit to the end. But he knew the danger there. His only alternative, however, was to rise and press through the enraptured crowd, which certainly would have resented the interruption. It seemed better to wait, and go out during the noisy applause that was sure to follow.

At the second verse Hamilton, still singing, came nearer. A path opened before him, as before an inspired prophet. It was only Monte who moved his chair slightly and made ready. Still there was nothing he could do until the man committed some overt act. When Hamilton concluded his song, he was less than two feet away. By then Monte was on his feet. As the applause swept from every corner of the room, Hamilton seized from a near-by table a glass of wine, and, raising it, shouted a toast:—

"To the bride."

The crowd followed his eyes to the shrinking girl behind Monte. In good humor they rose, to a man, and joined in, draining their glasses. It was Monte's opportunity. Taking Marjory's arm, he started for the door.

But Hamilton was madder than he had ever been. He ran forward, laughing hysterically.

"Kiss the bride," he called.

This he actually attempted. Monte had only his left arm, and it was not his strongest; but back of it he felt a new power. He took Hamilton beneath the chin, and with a lurch the man fell sprawling over a table among the glasses. In the screaming confusion that followed, Monte fought his way to the door, using his shoulders and a straight arm to clear a path. In another second he had lifted Marjory into a cab.

Leaning forward, she clutched his arm as the cab jumped ahead.

"I'm sorry I had to make a scene," he apologized. "I should n't have hit him, but—I saw red for a second."

She would never forget that picture of Monte standing by her side, his head erect, his arm drawn back for the second blow which had proved unnecessary. All the other faces surrounding her had faded into a smoky background. She had been conscious of him alone, and of his great strength. She had felt that moment as if his strength had literally been hers also. She could have struck out, had it been necessary.

"You did n't hurt your shoulder, did you?" she asked anxiously.

He did not know—it did not much matter. Had Hamilton actually succeeded in reaching her lips, he would have torn his wounded arm from the bandages and struck with that too. He had never realized until then what sacred things her lips were. He had known them only as beautiful. They were beautiful now as he looked down at them. Slightly parted, they held his eyes with a strange, new fascination. They were alive, those lips. They were warm and pulsating. He found himself breathing faster because of them. He seemed, against his will, to be bending toward them. Then, with a wrench, he tore himself free from the spell, not daring to look at her again.

Leaving her to Marie at the door of her room, Monte went into his own apartment. He threw open a window, and stood there in the dark with the cool night breeze blowing in upon him. After Maxim's, the more clean air the better; after what had followed in the cab, the more cool air the better.

He was still confused by it; still frightened by it. For a moment he had felt himself caught in the clutch of some power over which he had no control. That was the startling truth that stood out most prominently. He had been like one intoxicated—he who never before in his life had lost a grip upon himself. That fact struck at the very heart of his whole philosophy of life. Always normal—that had been his boast; never losing his head over this thing or that. It was the only way a man could keep from worrying. It was the only way a man could keep sane. The moment you wanted anything like the devil, then the devil was to pay. This evening he had proved that.

He went back to the affair at Maxim's. He should have known better than to take her there, anyway. She did not belong in such a place. She did not belong anywhere he had taken her to-day. To-morrow—but all this was beside the point.

The question that he would most like to answer at this moment was whether this last wild episode of Hamilton's was due to absinthe or to that same weird passion which a few weeks before had led the man to shoot. It had been beastly of Hamilton to try to reach her lips. That, doubtless, was the absinthe. It robbed him of his senses. But the look in the man's eyes when he sang, the awful hunger that burned in them when he gave his mad toast—those things seemed to spring from a different source. The man, in a room full of strangers, had seen only her, had sung only to her. Monte doubted if the crazed fellow saw even him. He saw no one but this one woman. That was madness—but it did not come of absinthe. The absinthe may have caused the final utter breakdown of Hamilton's self-control here and at Madame Courcy's—but that the desire could be there without it Monte had twice proved to himself that evening.

Once was when he had struck Hamilton. He alone knew that when he hit that time it was with the lust to kill—even as Hamilton had shot to kill. The feeling lasted only the fraction of a second—merely while his fist was plunging toward Hamilton's chin. But, however brief, it had sprung from within him—a blood-red, frenzied desire to beat down the other man. At the moment he was not so much conscious of trying to protect her as to rid himself of Hamilton.

The second mad moment had come in the cab, when he had looked down at her lips. As the passion to kill left him, another equally strong passion had taken its place. He had hungered for her lips—the very lips Hamilton, a moment before, had attempted to violate. He who all his life had looked as indifferently upon living lips as upon sculptured lips had suddenly found himself in the clutch of a mighty desire. For a second he had swayed under the temptation. He had been ready to risk everything, because for a heartbeat or two nothing else seemed to matter. In his madness, he had even dared think that delicate, sensitive mouth trembled a like desire.

Even here in the dark, alone, something of the same desire returned. He began to pace the room.

How she would have hated him had he yielded to that impulse! He shuddered as he pictured the look of horror that would have leaped into her dark eyes. Then she would have shrunk away frightened, and her eyes would have grown cold—those eyes that had only so lately warmed at all. Her face would have turned to marble—the face that only so lately had relaxed.

She trusted him—trusted him to the extent of being willing to marry him to save herself from the very danger with which he had threatened her. Except that at the last moment he had resisted, he was no better than Hamilton.

In her despair she had cried, "Why won't they let me alone?" And he had urged her to come with him, so that she might be let alone. He was to be merely her *camarade de voyage*—her big brother. Then, in less than twelve hours, he had become like the others. He felt unfit to remain in the next room to her—unfit to greet her in the morning. In an agony of remorse, he clenched his fists.

He drew himself up shortly. A new question leaped to his brain. Was this, then, love? The thought brought both solace and fresh terror. It gave him at least some justification for his moment of temptation; but it also brought vividly before him countless new dangers. If this were love, then he must face day after day of this sort of thing. Then he would be at the mercy of a passion that must inevitably lead him either to Hamilton's plight or to Chic Warren's equally unenviable position. Each man, in his own way, paid the cost: Hamilton, mad at Maxim's; Chic pacing the floor, with beaded brow, at night. With these two examples before him, surely he should have learned his lesson. Against them he could place his own normal life—ten years of it without a single hour such as these hours through which he was now living.

That was because he had kept steady. Ambition, love, drunkenness, gluttony—these were all excesses. His own father had desired mightily to be governor of a State, and it had killed him; his grandfather had died amassing the Covington fortune; he had friends who had died of love, and others who had overdrunk and overeaten. The secret of happiness was not to want anything you did not have. If you went beyond that, you paid the cost in new sacrifices, leading again to sacrifices growing out of those.

Monte lighted a cigarette and inhaled a deep puff. The thing for him to do was fairly clear: to pack his bag and leave while he still retained the use of his reasoning faculties. He had been swept off his feet for an instant, that was all. Let him go on with his schedule for a month, and he would recover his balance.

The suggestion was considerably simplified by the fact that it was not necessary to consider Marjory in any way. He would be in no sense deserting her, because she was in no way dependent upon him. She had ample funds of her own, and Marie for company. He had not married her because of any need she had for him along those lines. The protection of his name she would still have. As Mrs. Covington she could travel as safely without him as with him. Even Hamilton was eliminated. He had received his lesson. Anyway, she would probably leave Paris at once for Étois, and so be out of reach of Hamilton.

Monte wondered if she would miss him. Perhaps, for a day or so; but, after all, she would have without him the same wider freedom she craved. She would have all the advantages of a widow without the necessity of admitting that her husband was dead. He would always be in the background—an invisible guard. It was odd that neither she nor he had considered that as an attractive possibility. It was decidedly more practical than the present arrangement.

As for himself, he was ready to admit frankly that after to-day golf on an English course would for a time be a bore. From the first sight of her this morning until now, he had not had a dull moment. She had taken him back to the days when his emotions had been quick to respond to each day as a new adventure in life.

It was last winter in Davos that he had first begun to note the keen edge of pleasure becoming the least bit dulled. He had followed the routine of his amusements almost mechanically. He had been conscious of a younger element there who seemed to crowd in just ahead of him. Some of them were young ladies he remembered having seen with pig-tails. They smiled saucily at him—with a confidence that suggested he was no longer to be greatly feared. He could remember when they blushed shyly if he as much as glanced in their direction. His schedule had become a little too much of a schedule. It suggested the annual tour of the middle-aged gentlemen who follow the spas and drink of the waters.

He felt all those things now even more keenly than he had at the time. Looking back at them, he gained a new perspective that emphasized each disagreeable detail. But he had only to think of Marjory as there with him and—presto, they vanished. Had she been with him at Davos—better still, were she able to go to Davos with him next winter—he knew with what joy she would sit in front of him on the bob-sled and take the breathless dip of the Long Run. He knew how she would meet him in the morning with her cheeks stung into a deep red by the clean cold of the mountain air. She would climb the heights with him, laughing. She would skate with him and ski with him, and there would be no one younger than they.

Monte again began to pace his room. She must go to Davos with him next winter. He must take her around the whole schedule with him. She must go to England and golf with him, and from there to his camp. She would love it there. He could picture her in the woods, on the lake, and before the camp-fire, beneath the stars.

From there they would go on to Cambridge for the football season. She would like that. As a girl she had been cheated of all the big games, and he would make up for it. So they would go on to New York for the holidays. He had had rather a stupid time of it last year. He had gone down to Chic's for Christmas, but had been oppressed by an uncomfortable feeling that he did not belong there. Mrs. Chic had been busy with so many presents for others that he had felt like old Scrooge. He had made his usual gifts to relatives, but only as a matter of habit. With Marjory with him, he would be glad to go shopping as Chic and Mrs. Chic did. He might even go on to Philadelphia with her and look up some of the relatives he had lately been avoiding.

Where in thunder had his thoughts taken him again? He put his head in his hands. He had carried her around his whole schedule with him just as if this were some honest-to-God marriage. He had done this while she lay in the next room peacefully sleeping in perfect trust.

She must never know this danger, nor be further subjected to it. There was only one safe way—to take the early train for Calais without even seeing her again.

Monte sat down at the writing-desk and seized a pen.

Dear Marjory [he began]: Something has come up unexpectedly that makes it necessary for me to take an early train for England. I can't tell how long I shall be gone, but that of course is not important. I hope you will go on to Étois, as we had planned; or, at any rate, leave Paris. Somehow, I feel that you belong out under the blue sky and not in town.

He paused a moment and read over that last sentence. Then he scratched it out. Then he tore up the whole letter.

What he had to say should be not written. He must meet her in the morning and tell her like a man.

CHAPTER XI
A CANCELED RESERVATION

Though it was late when he retired, Monte found himself wide awake at half past seven. Springing from bed, he took his cold tub, shaved, and after dressing proceeded to pack his bags. The process was simple; he called the hotel valet, gave the order to have them ready as soon as possible, and went below. From the office he telephoned upstairs to Marie, and learned that madame would meet him in the breakfast-room at nine. This left him a half-hour in which to pay his bill at the hotel, order a reservation on the express to Calais, and buy a large bunch of fresh violets, which he had placed on the breakfast table—a little table in a sunshiny corner.

Monte was calmer this morning than he had been the night before. He was rested; the interval of eight hours that had passed since he last saw her gave him, however slight, a certain perspective, while his normal surroundings, seen in broad daylight, tended to steady him further. The hotel clerk, busy about his uninspired duties; the impassive waiters in black and white; the solid-looking Englishmen and their wives who began to make their appearance, lent a sense of unreality to the events of yesterday.

Yet, even so, his thoughts clung tenaciously to the necessity of his departure. In a way, the very normality of this morning world emphasized that necessity. He recalled that it was to just such a day as this he had awakened, yesterday. The hotel clerk had been standing exactly where he was now, sorting the morning mail, stopping every now and then with a troubled frown to make out an indistinct address. The corpulent porter in his blue blouse stood exactly where he was now standing, jealously guarding the door. Vehicles had been passing this way and that on the street outside. He had heard the same undertone of leisurely moving life—the scuffling of feet, the closing of doors, distant voices, the rumble of traffic. Then, after this lazy prelude, he had been swept on and on to the final dizzy climax.

That must not happen again. At this moment he knew he had a firm grip on himself—but at this moment yesterday he had felt even more secure. There had been no past then. That seemed a big word to use for such recent events covering so few hours; and yet it was none too big. It covered nothing less than the revelation of a man to himself. If that process sometimes takes years, it is none the less significant if it takes place in a day.

"Good-morning, Monte."

He turned quickly—so quickly that she started in surprise.

"Is anything the matter?" she asked.

She was in blue this morning, and wore at an angle a broad-brimmed hat trimmed with black and white. He thought her eyes looked a trifle tired. He would have said she had not slept well.

"I—I didn't know you were down," he faltered.

The interval of six hours upon which he had been depending vanished instantly. To-day was but the continuation of yesterday. As he moved toward the breakfast-room at her side, the outside world disappeared as by magic, leaving only her world—the world immediately about her, which she dominated. This room which she entered by his side was no longer merely the salle-à-manger of the Normandie. He was conscious of no portion of it other than that which included their table. All the sunshine in the world concentrated into the rays that fell about her.

He felt this, and yet at the same time he was aware of the absurdity of such exaggeration. It was the sort of thing that annoyed him when he saw it in others. All those newly married couples he used to meet on the German liners were afflicted in this same way. Each one of them acted as if the ship were their ship, the ocean their ocean, even the blue sky and the stars at night their sky and their stars. When he was in a good humor, he used to laugh at this; when in a bad humor, it disgusted him.

"Monte," she said, as soon as they were seated, "I was depending upon you this morning."

She studied him a second, and then tried to smile, adding quickly:—

"I don't like you to disappoint me like this."

"What do you mean?" he asked nervously.

She frowned, but it was at herself, not at him. It did not do much except make dimples between her brows.

"I lay awake a good deal last night—thinking," she answered.

"Good Lord!" he exclaimed. "You ought n't to have done that!"

"It was n't wise," she admitted. "But I looked forward to the daylight—and you—to bring me back to normal."

"Well, here we are," he hastened to assure her. "I had the sun up ready for you several hours ago."

"You—you look so serious."

She leaned forward.

"Monte," she pleaded, "you must n't go back on me like that—now. I suppose women can't help getting the fidgets once in a while and thinking all sorts of things. I was tired. I 'm not used to being so very gay. And I let myself go a little, because I thought in the morning I 'd find you the same old Monte. I 've known you so long, and you always *have* been the same."

"It was a pretty exciting day for both of us," he tried to explain.

"How for you?"

"Well, to start with, one does n't get married every morning."

He saw her cheeks flush. Then she drew back.

"I think we ought to forget that as much as possible," she told him.

Here was his opportunity. The way to forget—the only way—was for him to continue with his interrupted schedule to England, and for her to go on alone to Étois. It was not too late for that—if he started at once. Surely it ought to be the matter of only a few weeks to undo a single day. Let him get the tang of the salt air, let him go to bed every night dog-tired physically, let him get out of sight of her eyes and lips, and that something—intangible as a perfume—that emanated from her, and doubtless he would be laughing at himself as heartily as he had laughed at others.

But he could not frame the words. His lips refused to move. Not only that, but, facing her here, it seemed a grossly brutal thing to do. She looked so gentle and fragile this morning as, picking up the violets, she half hid her face in them.

"You mean we ought to go back to the day before yesterday?" he asked.

"In our thoughts," she answered.

"And forget that we are—"

She nodded quickly, not allowing him to finish.

"Because," she explained, "I think it must be that which is making you serious. I don't know you that way. It is n't you. I 've seen you all these years, wandering around wherever your fancy took you—care-free and smiling. I've always envied you, and now—I thought you were just going to keep right on, only taking me with you. Is n't that what we planned?"

"Yes," he nodded. "We started yesterday."

"I shall never forget that part of yesterday," she said.

"It was n't so bad, except for Hamilton."

"It was n't so bad even with Hamilton," she corrected. "I don't think I can ever be afraid of him again."

"Then it was n't he that bothered you last night?" he asked quickly.

"No," she answered.

"It—it was n't I?"

She laughed uneasily.

"No, Monte; because you were just yourself yesterday."

He wondered about that. He wondered, if he placed before her all the facts, including the hours after he left her, if she would have said that. Here was his second opportunity to tell her what he had planned. If he did not intend to go on, he should speak now. To-morrow it would be too late. By noon it would be too late. By the time they finished their breakfast, it would be too late.

He met her eyes. They were steady as planets. They were honest and clear and clean and confident. They trusted him, and he knew it. He took a deep breath and leaned forward. Impulsively she leaned across the table and placed her hand upon his.

"Dear old Monte," she breathed.

It was too late—now! He saw her in a sort of mist of dancing golden motes. He felt the steady throb of her pulse.

She withdrew her hand as quickly as she had given it. It was as if she did not dare allow it to remain there. It was that which made him smile with a certain confidence of his own.

"What we'd better do," he said, "is to get out of Paris. I'm afraid the pace here is too hot for us."

"To Étois?" she asked.

"That's as good a place as any. Could you start this afternoon?"

"If you wish."

"The idea is to move on as soon as you begin to think," he explained, with his old-time lightness. "Of course, the best way is to walk. If you can't walk—why, the next best thing—"

He paused a moment to consider a new idea. It was odd that it had never occurred to him before.

"I have it!" he continued. "We'll go to Étois by motor. It's a beautiful drive down there. I made the trip alone three years ago in a car I owned. We'll take our time, putting up at the little villages along the way. We'll let the sun soak into us. We'll get away from people. It's people who make you worry. I have a notion it will be good for us both. This Hamilton episode has left us a bit morbid. What we need is something to bring us back to normal."

"I'd love it," she fell in eagerly. "We'll just play gypsy."

"Right. Now, what you want to do is to throw into a dress-suitcase a few things, and we'll ship the trunks by rail to Nice. All you need is a toothbrush, a change of socks, and—"

"There's Marie," she interrupted.

"Can't we ship her by rail too?"

"No, Monte," she answered, with a decided shake of her head.

"But, hang it all, people don't go a-gypsying with French maids!"

"Why not?" she demanded.

She asked the question quite honestly. He had forgotten Marie utterly until this moment, and she seemed to join the party like an intruder. Always she would be upon the back seat.

"Wouldn't you feel freer without her?" he asked.

"I should n't feel at all proper," she declared.

"Then we might just as well not have been married."

"Only," she laughed, "if we had n't taken that precaution it would n't have been proper for me to go, even with Marie."

"I'm glad we've accomplished something, anyhow," he answered good-naturedly.

"We've accomplished a great deal," she assured him. "Yesterday morning I could n't—at this time—have done even the proper things and felt proper. Oh, you don't know how people look at you, and how that look makes you feel, even when you know better. I could n't have sat here at breakfast with you and felt comfortable. Now we can sit here and plan a wonderful trip like this. It's all because you're just Monte."

"And you just you!"

"Only I don't count for anything. It makes me feel even more selfish than I am."

"Don't count?" he exclaimed. "Why—"

He stifled the words that sprang to his lips. It was only because she thought she did not count that she was able to feel comfortable. Once let her know that she counted as at that moment she did count to him, and even what little happiness he was able to bring her would vanish. He would be to her then merely one of the others—even as he was to himself.

He rose abruptly.

"I must see about getting a machine," he said. "I want to start this afternoon if possible."

"I'll be ready," she agreed.

As they went out to the office, the clerk stepped up to him.

"I have secured the reservation, monsieur," he announced.

"Please cancel it," replied Monte.

"Reservation?" inquired Marjory.

"On the Calais express—for a friend of mine who has decided not to go," he answered.

CHAPTER XII
A WEDDING JOURNEY

Monte made an extravagant purchase: a new high-powered touring car capacious enough for a whole family—his idea being, that the roomier the car, the less Marie would show up in it. On the other hand, if he cared to consider her in that way, Marie would be there as much for his protection as Marjory's. The task that lay ahead of him this next week was well defined; it was to get back to normal. He had diagnosed his disease—now he must cure it. It would have been much easier to have done this by himself, but this was impossible. He must learn to gaze steadily into her eyes, while gazing into them; he must learn to look indifferently upon her lips, with her within arm's reach of him. Here was a man's job.

He was not even to have the machine to occupy his attention; for there was no time to secure a license, and so he must take with him a chauffeur. He was fortunate in being able to secure one on the spot—Louis Santerre, a good-looking lad with the best of recommendations. He ordered him to be at the hotel at three.

Thus, in less than an hour from the time he entered the salesroom, Monte had bought and paid for his car, hired his man, given orders for certain accessories, and left, with Monsieur Mansart bowing him out and heartily wishing that all his customers were of this type.

There were, however, several little things that Monte still wished to purchase—an automobile coat and cap, for one thing; also some rugs. These he found in a near-by store. It was as he was leaving that the clerk—who, it seems, must have had an eye—noticed the shiny new gold ring upon Monte's left hand.

"Madame is well supplied?" he inquired.

"Madame? Who the devil is madame?" demanded Monte.

"Pardon, monsieur," replied the clerk in some confusion, fearing he had made a grave mistake. "I did not know monsieur was traveling alone."

Then it was Monte's turn to show signs of confusion. It was quite true he was not traveling alone. It was the truest thing he knew just then.

"What is necessary for a lady traveling by motor?" he inquired.

The clerk would take great pleasure in showing him in a department devoted to that very end. It was after one bewildering glance about the counters that he became of the opinion that his question should have been: "What is it that a lady does not wear when traveling by motor?" He saw coats and bonnets and goggles and vanity boxes and gloves, to mention only a few of those things he took in at first glance.

"We are leaving in some haste," explained Monte, "so I'm afraid she has none of these things. Would n't the easiest way be for you to give me one of each?"

That indeed would be a pleasure. Did monsieur know the correct size?

Only in a general way—madame was not quite his height and weighed in the neighborhood of one hundred and fifty pounds. That was enough to go upon for outside garments. Still there remained a wide choice of style and color. In this Monte pleased himself, pointing his stick with sure judgment at what took his fancy, as this and the other thing was placed before him. It was a decidedly novel and a very pleasant occupation.

In this way he spent the best part of another hour, and made a payment in American Express orders of a considerable sum. That, however, involved nothing but tearing from the book he always carried as many orders for twenty-five dollars as most nearly approximated the sum total. The articles were to be delivered within one hour to "Madame M. Covington, Hôtel Normandie."

Monte left the store with a sense of satisfaction, tempered a trifle by an uncomfortable doubt as to just how this presumption on his part would be received. However, he was well within his rights. He held sturdily to that.

With still two hours before he could return,—for he must leave her free until luncheon,—he went on to the Champs Élysées and so to the Bois. He still dwelt with pleasure upon the opportunity that had been offered him to buy those few things for her. It sent him along briskly with a smile on his face. It did more; it suggested a new idea. The reason he had been taking himself so seriously was that he had been thinking too much about himself and not enough about her. The simple way out of that difficulty was from now on not to consider himself at all. After all, what happened to him did not much matter, as long as it did not affect her. His job from now on was to make her happy.

For the rest of his walk he kept tight hold of that idea, and came back to the hotel with a firm grip on it. He called to her through the door of her room:—

"How you making it?"

"Pretty well," came her voice. "Only I went shopping and bought all my things—including a coat for you. Then, when I return, I find a whole boxful from you."

"All my efforts wasted!" he exclaimed.

"No, Monte," she replied quickly. "I could n't allow that, because—well, because it was so thoughtful of you. So I kept the coat and bonnet you selected—and a few other things. I've just sent Marie out to return the rest."

She had kept the coat and bonnet that he selected! What in thunder was there about that to make a man feel so confoundedly well satisfied?

They left the hotel at three, and rode that day as far as a country inn which took their fancy just before coming into Joigny. It was, to Marjory, a wonderful ride—a ride that made her feel that with each succeeding mile she was leaving farther and farther behind her every care she had ever had in the world. It was a ride straight into the heart of a green country basking sleepily beneath blue skies; of contented people going about their pleasant tasks; of snug, fat farms and snug little houses, with glimpses of an occasional chateau in the background.

When Monte held out his hand to assist her down, she laughed light-heartedly, refreshed in body and soul. For Monte had been himself ever since they started—better than himself. He had humored her every mood, allowing her to talk when she had felt like talking, or to sit back with her eyes half closed when she wished to give herself up to lazy content. Often, too, he had made her laugh with his absurd remarks—laugh spontaneously, as a child laughs. She had never seen him in such good humor, and could not remember when she herself had been in such good humor.

The rays of the sun were falling aslant as she stepped out, and the western sky was aglow with crimson and purple and pink. It was a drowsy world, with sounds grown distant and the perfume and color of the flowers grown nearer. At the door of the inn, which, looked as if it must have been standing right there in the days of dashing cavaliers, the proprietor and his wife were obsequiously bowing a welcome. It was not often that the big machines deigned to rest here.

Monte stepped toward them.

"Madame desires to rest here for the night, if accommodations may be secured," he said.

For the night? Mon Dieu! The proprietor had reckoned upon only a temporary sojourn—for a bottle of wine, perhaps. He had never entertained such a host as this. How many rooms would be required?

"Four," answered Monte.

"Let me see; monsieur and madame could be put in the front room."

Monte shook his head.

"Madame will occupy the front room alone," he informed him.

"Eh? Oh, I understand; a sister. That was a curious mistake. Eh bien, madame in the front room. Monsieur in the room to the right. The maid in the room on the back. But there is the chauffeur."

There was no room left for him, or for the machine either.

"Then he can go on to Joigny," announced Monte.

So Louis went on, and in less than five minutes the others were safely sorted out and tucked away in their respective rooms.

"We ought to get out and see the sun set," Monte called to Marjory as she waved him an adieu at her door.

"I'll be down in ten minutes," she nodded.

There is a princess latent in every woman. She makes her appearance early, and too often vanishes early. Not many women have the good fortune to see her—except perhaps for a few brief moments—after seventeen. But, however, far in the background, she remains as at least a romantic possibility as long as any trace of romance itself remains. She is a languid, luxury-loving creature, this princess; an Arabian Nights princess of silks and satins and perfumed surroundings. Through half-closed eyes she looks out upon a world of sunshine and flowers, untroubled as the fairy folk. Every one does her homage, and she in her turn smiles graciously, and there is nought else for her to do except to rest and be amused.

For a moment, here in the twilight, this princess returned to Marjory. As she sat before the mirror, doing over her hair, she held her chin a little higher at the thought and smiled at herself contentedly. She used to do just this—and feel ashamed of herself afterward—long, long ago, after she first met Monte at the Warrens'. For it was he who then had been her gallant knight, without which no one may be a fairy-book princess. He had just finished his college course, and eager-eyed was about to travel over the wide world. He was big and buoyant and handsome, and even more irresponsible then than now.

She recalled how one evening they sat alone upon the porch of the Warren house until late, and he had told her of his proposed journey. She had listened breathlessly, with her chin in her hands and her eyes big. When she came in, Mrs. Warren had placed an arm about her and looked significantly at her flushed cheeks and said gently:—

"Be careful, my dear. Don't you let that careless young prince take away your heart with him. Remember, he has not yet seen the world."

He had sailed away for a year and a day soon after this; and, perhaps because he was safely out of her life, she had allowed herself more liberty with him than otherwise she would have done. At any rate, that year she was a princess and he her prince.

Now, to-night, he came back for a little. It was the twilight, which deals gently with harsh realities, and the perfume of the flowers floating in at the open window, and the old room, doubtless. Only yesterday he called her "Your Highness," and she had not responded. There in the Café Riche none of her old dreams had returned. Perhaps it was because all her surroundings there had been too grossly real. That was no setting for a fairy prince, and a fairy prince was, of course, all he had ever been or was now. He was only for the world when the sun was low.

Outside her window she heard a voice:—

"Oh, Marjory."

She started. It was her prince calling. It was bewildering to have dreams suddenly blended with life itself. It was bewildering also to have the thoughts of seventeen suddenly blended with the realities of twenty-seven. She remained silent, breathing gently, as if afraid of being discovered.

"Marjory," he called again.

"Coming," she answered, with a quiet intake of breath.

Hatless and with a silk shawl over her shoulders, she hurried to where he was waiting. He too was hatless, even as he had been that night long ago when he had sat beside her. Something, too, of the same light of youth was in his eyes now as then.

Side by side they strolled through the quaint village of stone houses and to the top of a near-by hill, where they found themselves looking down upon Joigny outlined against the hazy tints of the pink-and-gold horizon.

"Oh, it's beautiful!" she exclaimed enthusiastically. "It's a fairy world."

"Better; it's a real world," he answered.

"I doubt it, Monte," she disagreed, with a touch of regret. "It's too perfect."

It would not last. It would begin to fade in a moment, even as her fairy prince would fade and become just Monte. She knew from the past. Besides, it was absolutely essential that this should not last. If it did—why, that would be absurd. It would be worse. It made her uncomfortable even to imagine this possibility for a moment, thus bringing about the very condition most unfavorable for fairy princes. For, if there is one advantage they have over ordinary princes, it is the gift of keeping their princesses always happy and content.

Somewhat shyly she glanced up at Monte. He was standing with his uninjured hand thrust into the pocket of his Norfolk jacket, staring fixedly at the western sky as if he had lost himself there. She thought his face was a bit set; but, for all that, he looked this moment more as she had known him at twenty-one than when he came back at twenty-two. After his travels of a year he had seemed to her so much wiser than she that he had instantly become her senior. She had listened to him as to a man of the world, with something of awe. It was more difficult then to have him for a prince, because princes, though brave and adventurous, must not be too wise.

She smiled as she realized that, as he stood there now, Monte did not in the least inspire her with awe or fear or a sense of superior wisdom. The mellow light softened his features and the light breeze had tousled his hair, so that for all his years told he might have been back in his football days. He had been like that all the afternoon.

A new tenderness swept over her. She would have liked to reach up her hand and smooth away the little puzzled frown between his brows. She almost dared to do it. Then he turned.

"You're right," he said, with a shrug of his shoulders. "It is n't real. See, it's fading now."

The pink clouds were turning a dull gray.

"Perhaps it's better it should," she suggested. "If it stayed like that all the time, we'd get so used to it we would n't see it."

He took out his watch.

"I ordered supper to be ready in a half hour," he said. "We'd better get back."

She fell in step by his side—by the side of her fairy prince. For, oddly enough, he had not begun to fade as the sunset faded. The twilight was deepening into the hushed night—a wonderful night that was like beautiful music heard at a distance. It left her scarcely conscious of moving. In the sky the stars were becoming clearer; in the houses, candles were beginning to twinkle. It was difficult to tell which were which—as if the sky and the earth were one.

There was no abrupt change even when they came into the inn, where near the open window a table had been set and two candles were burning.

"Oh," she exclaimed again, "here is another bit of fairy world."

He laughed abruptly.

"I hope the supper is real, anyhow," he said.

He spoke as if making a conscious effort to break the spell. It made her glance up as he seated her; but all she thought of then was that she would like to smooth back his hair. The spell was not broken.

Chops and cauliflower and a salad were served to them, with patties of fresh butter and crusted white bread. She was glad to see him eat heartily. She prepared his salad with a dash of salt and pepper, a little vinegar and oil. That much, at least, she was at liberty to do for him. It gave her a new pleasure.

"Monte," she asked, "do you suppose it's always as nice as this here?"

"If it were, would you like to stay?" he asked.

She thought a moment over that. Would it be possible just to drift on day after day, with Monte always a fairy prince beside her? She glanced up and met his eyes.

"I—I guess it's best to follow our schedule," she decided, with a little gasp.

CHAPTER XIII
A WEDDING JOURNEY (*continued*)

Through the golden sunshine and beneath the blue sky, they went on the next day, until with a nod she chose her place to stop for lunch, until with another nod, as the sun was getting low, she chose her place to stop for the night. This time they did not ask to know even the name of the village. It was his suggestion.

"Because," he explained, "that makes it seem as if we were trying to get somewhere. And we are n't, are we?"

"Wherever we are, we are," she nodded gayly.

"It is n't even important that we get to Étois," he insisted.

"Not in the slightest," she agreed. "Only, if we keep on going we'll get to the sea, won't we?"

"Then we can either skirt the shore or take a boat and cross the sea. It's all one."

"All one! You make me feel as if I had wings."

"Then you're happy?"

"Very, very happy, Monte. And you?"

"Yes," he answered abruptly.

She had no reason to doubt it. That night, as she sat alone in her room, she reviewed this day in order to satisfy herself on this point; for she felt a certain obligation. He had given to her so generously that the least she in her turn could do was to make sure that he was comfortable and content. That, all his life, was the most he had asked for. It was the most he asked for now. He must wake each morning free of worries, come down to a good breakfast and find his coffee hot, have a pleasant time of it during the day without being bored, and end with a roast and salad and later a good bed. These were simple desires—thoroughly wholesome, normal desires. With the means at his command, with the freedom from restraint that had been his ever since he left college, it was a great deal to his credit that he had been able to retain such modest tastes. He had been at liberty to choose what he wished, and he had chosen decently.

This morning she had come down early and looked to his coffee herself. It was a slight thing, but she had awakened with a desire to do something positive and personal for him. She had been satisfied when he exclaimed, without knowing the part she played in it:—

"This coffee is bully!"

It had started the day right and given her a lightness of spirit that was reflected in her talk and even in her smiles. She had smiled from within. She was quite sure that the day had been a success, and that so far, at any rate, Monte had not been either bored or worried. Sitting there in the dark, she felt strangely elated over the fact. She had been able to send her fairy prince to his sleep contented. It gave her a motherly feeling of a task well done. After all, Monte was scarcely more than a boy.

Her thoughts went back to the phrase he had used at the end of the day's journey.

"We aren't getting anywhere, are we?" he had asked.

At the moment she had not thought he meant anything more than he said. He seldom did. It was restful to know that she need never look for hidden meanings in his chance remarks. He meant only that there was no haste; that it made no difference when they reached this town or that.

They had no destination.

That was true, and yet the thought disturbed her a trifle. It did not seem quite right for Monte to have no destination. He was worth something more than merely to revolve in a circle. He should have a Holy Grail. Give him something to fight for, and he would fight hard. Twice to-day she had caught a light in his eyes that had suggested this to her—a clean, white light that had hinted of a Monte with a destination. But would not that destroy the very poise that made him just Monte?

It was too puzzling a question for her own peace of mind. She turned away from it and slowly began to take down her hair.

On and on they went the third day—straight on—with their destination still hidden. That night, when again alone, she sat even longer by her open window than she had yesterday, instead of going to bed and to sleep, which would have been the sensible thing to do. In some ways this had been rather a more exciting day than the others. Again she had risen early and come down to order his coffee; but he too must have risen early, for he had come upon her as she was giving her instructions. It had been an embarrassing moment for her, and she had tried to carry it off with a laugh. That she was not to do so surprised her and added a still deeper flush to her cheeks.

"So this is the secret of my good coffee?" he asked.

"There is so very little I can do for you," she faltered.

"That is a whole lot more than I deserve," he answered.

However, he was pleased by this trivial attention, and she knew it. It was an absurdly insignificant incident, and yet here she was recalling it with something like a thrill. Not only that, but she recalled another and equally preposterous detail of the day. She had dropped her vanity-box in the car, and as they both stooped for it his cheek had brushed hers. He laughed lightly and apologized—forgetting it the next second. Eight hours later she dared remember it, like any schoolgirl. Small wonder that she glanced about to make sure the room was empty. It sent her to bed shamefaced.

The fourth day came, with the golden road still unfolding before them and her fairy prince still beside her. Then the fifth day, and that night they stopped within sight of the ocean. It came as a surprise to both of them. It was as if, after all, they had reached a destination, when as a matter of fact they had done nothing of the sort. It meant, to be sure, that the next day would find them in Nice, which would end their ride, because they intended to remain there for a day or two until they arranged for a villa in Étois, which, being in the mountains, they must reach afoot. But if she did not like it she had only to nod and they could move on to somewhere else. There was nothing final even about Étois.

That evening they walked by the shore of the sea, and Monte appeared quieter than usual.

"I have wired ahead for rooms at the Hôtel des Roses," he announced.

"Yes, Monte," she said.

"It's where I've stopped for ten years. The last time I was there I found Edhart gone, and was very uncomfortable."

"You were as dependent upon him as that?" she asked.

"It was what lured me on to Paris—and you," he smiled.

"Then I must be indebted to Edhart also."

"I think it would be no more than decent to look up his grave and place a wreath of roses there," he observed.

"But, Monte," she protested, "I should hate to imagine he had to give up his life—for just this."

"At any rate, if he hadn't died I'm sure I should have kept to my schedule," he said seriously.

"And then?"

"I should not have been here."

"You speak regretfully?" she asked.

He stopped abruptly and seized her arm.

"You know better," he answered.

For a moment she looked dizzily into his eyes. Then he broke the tension by smiling.

"I guess we'd better turn back," he said below his breath.

It was evident that Monte was not quite himself at that moment. That night she heard the roll of the ocean as she tried to sleep, and it said many strange things to her. She did not sleep well.

The next morning they were on their way again, reaching the Hôtel des Roses at six in the afternoon. Henri was at the door to meet them. Henri, he thought, had greatly improved since his last visit. Perhaps Edhart, from his seat on high, had been instructing him. The man seemed to understand better without being told what Monsieur Covington desired. The apartments were ready, and it was merely a personal matter between Monte and the garçon to have his trunk transferred from the second floor to the third and Marie's trunk brought down from the third to the second. Even Edhart might have been pardoned for making this mistake in the distribution of the luggage, if not previously informed.

That evening Marjory begged to be excused from dinner, and Monte dined alone. He dined alone in the small salle-à-manger where he had always dined alone, and where the last time he was here he had grown in an instant from twenty-two to thirty-two. Now, in another instant, it was as if he had gone back to twenty-two. It was even almost as if Edhart had returned to life. The mellow glow of the long twilight tinted the room just as it used to do. Across the boulevard he saw the Mediterranean, languid and blue.

A thing that impressed Monte was how amazingly friendly every one was—how amazingly friendly even the material objects were. His old table in the corner had been reserved for him, but this time it had been arranged for two. The empty chair opposite him was quite as friendly as Marjory herself might have been. It kept him company and humored his thoughts. It said, as plainly as it is possible for a chair to speak:—

"Madame Covington is disappointed to think she could not join you this evening, but you must remember that it is not to be expected of a woman to stand these long journeys like a man. However, she will have breakfast with you in the morning. That is something to look forward to. In the meanwhile let me serve to remind you that she is upstairs—upstairs in the room you used to occupy. Perhaps even at this moment she is looking out the window at this same languid blue sea. Being up there, she is within call. Should you need her—really need her—you may be perfectly sure that she would come to you.

"That time you were ill here two years ago, you had rather a bad time of it because there was no one to visit you except a few chance acquaintances about whom you did not care. Well, it would not be like that now. She would sit by your bed all night long and all day long, too, if you permitted. She is that kind. So, you see, you are really not dining alone to-night. I, though only an empty chair, am here to remind you of that."

Felix, who was in charge of the salle-à-manger, hovered near Monte as if he felt the latter to be his especial charge. He served as Monte's right hand—the hand of the sling. He was very much disturbed because madame refused her dinner, and every now and then thought of something new that possibly might tempt her.

Every one else about the hotel was equally friendly, racking his brains to find a way of serving Monte by serving madame. It made him feel quite like those lordly personages who used to come here with a title and turn the place topsy-turvy for themselves and for their women-folk. He recalled a certain count of something who arrived with his young wife and who in a day had half of Nice in his service. Monte felt like him, only more so. There was a certain obsequiousness that the count demanded which vanished the moment his back was turned; but the interest of Felix and his fellows now was based upon something finer than fear. Monte felt it had to do with Marjory herself, and also—well, in a sense she was carrying a title too. She was, to these others, a bride.

But it was a great relief to know that she was not the sort of bride of which he had seen too many in the last ten years. It would be a pleasure to show these fellows a bride who would give them no cause to smile behind their hands. He would show them a bride who could still conduct herself like a rational human being, instead of like a petulant princess or a moon-struck school girl.

Monte lighted a cigarette and went out upon the Quai Massena for a stroll. It was late in the season for the crowds. They had long since adjourned to the mountains or to Paris. But still there were plenty remaining. He would not have cared greatly had there been no one left. It was a relief to have the shore to himself. He had formerly been rather sensitive about being anywhere out of season. In fact, this was the first time he had ever been here later than May. But the difference was not so great as he had imagined it must be. Neither the night sky nor the great turquoise mirror beneath it appeared out of season.

Monte did not stray far. He walked contentedly back and forth for the matter of an hour. He might have kept on until midnight, had it not been for a messenger from the hotel who handed him a note. Indifferently he opened it and read:

I've gone to the Hôtel d'Angleterre. Please don't try to see me to-night. Hastily,

MARJORY.

CHAPTER XIV
THE BRIDE RUNS AWAY

Henri, who was greatly disturbed, explained to Monte that madame came downstairs shortly after monsieur left for his walk and asked for him. Being told that monsieur had gone out, she too had gone out, wearing a light shawl—to meet monsieur, as Henri supposed. In some fifteen minutes madame had returned, appearing somewhat excited, if it were permissible to say so. Thereupon she had given orders to have her luggage and the luggage of her maid removed at once to the Hôtel d'Angleterre. Henri had assured her that if her rooms were not suitable he would turn the house upside down to please her.

"No, no," she had answered; "it is not that. You are very kind, Henri."

He had then made so bold as to suggest that a messenger be sent out to find monsieur.

"By all means," she had answered. "I will give you a note to take to him."

She had sat down and written the note and Henri had dispatched it immediately. But, also immediately, madame and her maid had left.

"I beg monsieur to believe that if there is anything—"

Monte waved the man aside, went to the telephone, and rang up the Hôtel d'Angleterre.

"I wish to know if a Madame Covington has recently arrived."

"Non, monsieur," was the response.

"Look here," said Monte sharply. "Make sure of that. She must have reached there within fifteen minutes."

"We have had no arrivals here within that time except a Mademoiselle Stockton and her maid."

"Eh?" snapped Monte. "Repeat that again."

"Mademoiselle Stockton," the clerk obeyed.

"She signed the register with that name?"

"But yes. If monsieur—"

"All right; thanks."

"You found her?" inquired Henri solicitously.

"Yes," nodded Monte, and went out into the night again.

There was nothing he could do—absolutely nothing. She had given her orders, and they must be obeyed. He returned to the Quai Massena, to the shore of the sea; but he walked nervously now, in a world that, as far as he was concerned, was starless and colorless. He had thought at first, naturally enough, that Hamilton was in some way concerned; but he dismissed that now as wholly unplausible. Instead of running away, in that case, she would have sent for him. It was decidedly more likely that this was some strange whimsy springing from within herself.

In looking back at the last few days, he recalled now that upon several occasions she had acted in a way not quite like herself. Last night, for instance, she had been disturbed. Again, it was most unusual for her not to dine with him. He had accepted her excuse that she was tired; but now he blamed himself for not having seen through so artificial an excuse, for not having detected that something else was troubling her.

She had run away as if in fear. She had not dared even to talk over with him the cause for her uneasiness. And he—blind fool that he was—had not detected anything unusual. He had gone off mooning, leaving her to fight her own fight. He had been so confoundedly self-satisfied and content because she was here with him, where heretofore he had always been alone, that he had gone stony blind to her comfort. That was the crude fact.

However, accusing himself did not bring him any nearer an explanation of her strange conduct. She would not have left him unless she had felt herself in some danger. If Hamilton were eliminated, who then remained by whom she could feel menaced? Clearly it must be himself.

The conclusion was like a blow in the face. It stunned him for a moment, and then left his cheeks burning. If she had scuttled away from him like a frightened rabbit, it could be for only one reason; because he had not been able to conceal the truth. And he had thought that he had succeeded in keeping the danger to himself.

He turned in the direction of the Hôtel d'Angleterre. He did not intend to try to see her. He wished only to be a little nearer. Surely there was no harm in that. The boulevard had become deserted, and he was terribly lonesome out here alone. The old black dog that had pounced upon him in Paris came back and hugged him closer.

He squared his shoulders. He must shake himself free of that. The thing to keep in mind was that he did not count in this affair. She alone must be considered. If he had frightened her, he must find some way of reassuring her. He must take a tighter grip than ever upon himself, face her to-morrow, and laugh away her fears. He must do that, because he must justify her faith in him. That was all he had of her—her faith in him. If he killed that, then she would vanish utterly.

After this last week, to be here or anywhere else without her was unthinkable. He must make her believe that he took even this new development lightly. He must go to her in the morning as just Monte. So, if he were very, very careful, he might coax her back a little way into his life. That was not very much to hope for.

Monte was all wrong. From beginning to end, he was wrong. Marjory had run away, not from him, but from some one else. When she left the hotel she had been on her way to join monsieur, as Henri had correctly surmised. From her window she had been watching him for the matter of half an hour as he paced up and down the quay before the hotel. Every time Monte disappeared from sight at the end of a lap, she held her breath until he appeared again. Every time he appeared again, her heart beat faster. He seemed such a lonely figure that her conscience troubled her. He was so good, was Monte—so good and four-square.

She had left him to dine alone, and without a protest he had submitted. That was like him; and yet, if he had only as much as looked his disappointment, she would have dressed and come down. She had been ready to do so. It was only the initial excitement that prompted her at first to shut herself up. Coming to this hotel, where for ten years he had been coming alone, was almost like going back into his life for that length of time. Then, Monte had signed the register "Monsieur and Madame Covington." With bated breath she had watched him do it.

After that the roses in her room and the attention of every one to her as to a bride—all those things had frightened her at first. Yet she knew they were bowing low, not to her, but to Madame Covington. This was what made her ears burn. This was what made her seek the seclusion of her room. She felt like an imposter, claiming honors that did not belong to her. It made her so uncomfortable that she could not face even Marie. She sent her off.

Sitting by the open window, she watched Monte as he walked alone, with a queer little ache in her heart. How faithfully he had lived up to his bargain! He had given her every tittle of the freedom she had craved. In all things he had sought her wishes, asking nothing for himself. It was she who gave the order for starting every morning, for stopping at night. She chose this inn or that, as pleased her fancy. She talked when she wished to talk, and remained silent when she preferred. If, instead of coming to Nice and Étois, she had expressed a desire to turn in some other direction, she knew he would merely have nodded.

It was all one to him. East, west, north, or south—what was the odds? Married or single—what was the odds?

So she also should have felt. With this big man by her side to guard her and do her will, she should have been able to abandon herself utterly to the delights of each passing hour—to the magic of the fairy kingdom he had made for her. It was all she had asked for, and that much it was her right to accept, if he chose to give it. She was cheating no one. Monte himself would have been the first to admit that. Therefore she should have been quite at peace with herself.

The fact remained, however, that each day since they had left Paris she had found herself more and more at the mercy of strange moods; sometimes an unusual and inexplicable exhilaration, such as that moment last night when Monte had turned and seized her arm; sometimes an unnatural depression, like that which now oppressed her. These had been only intervals, to be sure. The hours between had been all she had looked forward to—warm, basking hours of lazy content.

To-night she had been longer than ever before in recovering her balance. She had expected to undress, go to bed, and so to sleep. Perhaps it was the sight of Monte pacing up and down there alone that prolonged her mood. Yet, not to see him, all that was necessary was to close her eyes or to turn the other way. It should have been easy to do this. Only it was not. She followed him back and forth. In some ways, a bride could not have acted more absurdly.

At the thought she withdrew from the window in startled confusion. Standing in the middle of the room, she stared about as if challenged as to her right there by some unseen visitor. This would never do. She was too much alone. She must go to Monte. He would set her right, because he understood. She would take his arm, his strong, steady arm, and walk a little way with him and laugh with him. That was what she needed.

She hurried into her clothes, struggling nervously with hooks and buttons as if there were need of haste. Then, throwing a light shawl over her shoulders, she went out past Henri, on her way to Monte.

Monte had been all wrong in his guesses. She had actually been running toward him instead of away from him when, just outside the hotel, she almost collided with Peter Noyes and his sister.

Peter Noyes did not see her at first. His eyes were covered with a green shade, even out here in the night. But his sister Beatrice gave an exclamation that brought him to attention and made him fumble at the shade as if to tear it off. Yet she had spoken but one word:—

"Marjory!"

She whose name had been called shrank back as if hoping the dark would hide her.

"Marjory!" cried Peter Noyes.

Beatrice rushed forward, seizing both the girl's hands.

"It is you," she exclaimed, as if Marjory sought to deny the fact. "Peter—Peter, it's Marjory Stockton!"

Peter stepped forward, his hand outstretched hesitatingly, as one who cannot see. Marjory took the hand, staring with questioning eyes at Beatrice.

"He worked too hard," explained the latter. "This is the price he paid."

"Oh, I'm sorry, Peter!" she cried.

He tried to smile.

"It's at moments like this I mind it," he answered. "I—I thought you were in Paris, Marjory."

"I came here to-day."

She spoke nervously.

"Then," he asked, "you—you are to be here a little while?"

Marjory passed her hand over her forehead.

"I don't know," she faltered.

Peter looked so thin! It was evident he had been long ill. She did not like to see him so. The shade over his eyes horrified her. Beatrice came nearer.

"If you could encourage him a little," she whispered. "He has wanted so much to see you."

It was as if she in some way were being held responsible.

"You're not stopping here?" gasped Marjory.

"At the Hôtel des Roses," nodded Beatrice. "And you?"

Peter with his haggard, earnest face, and Beatrice with her clear honest eyes, filled her with sudden shame. It would be impossible to make them understand. They were so American—so direct and uncompromising about such affairs as these.

Beatrice had the features of a Puritan maid, and dressed the part, from her severe little toque, her prim white dress reaching to her ankles, to her sturdy boots. Her blue eyes were already growing big at Marjory's hesitancy at answering so simple a question. She had been here once with Aunt Kitty—they had stopped at the Hôtel d'Angleterre. Marjory mumbled that name now.

"Then I may come over to-night to see you for a moment, may I not?" said Beatrice. "It is time Peter went in now."

"I—I may see you in the morning?" asked Peter.

"In the morning," she nodded. "Good-night."

She gave him her hand, and he held it as a child holds a hand in the dark.

"I'll be over in half an hour," Beatrice called back.

It was only a few blocks to the Hôtel d'Angleterre, but Marjory ran the distance. Happily the clerk remembered her, or she might have found some difficulty in having her excited excuse accepted that she was not quite suited at the Roses. Then back again to Henri and Marie she hurried, with orders to have the luggage transferred at once.

CHAPTER XV
IN THE DARK

In her new room at the Hôtel d'Angleterre, Marjory dismissed Marie and buried her hot face in her hands. She felt like a cornered thing—a shamed and cornered thing. She should not have given the name of the hotel. She should have sought Monte and ordered him to take her away. Only—she could not face Monte himself. She did not know how she was going to see him to-morrow—how she was ever going to see him again. "Monsieur and Madame Covington," he had signed the register. Beatrice must have seen it, but Peter had not. He must never see it, because he would force her to confess the truth—the truth she had been struggling to deny to herself.

She had trifled with a holy thing—that was the shameful truth. She had posed here as a wife when she was no wife. The ceremony at the English chapel helped her none. It only made her more dishonest. The memory of Peter Noyes had warned her at the time, but she had not listened. She had lacked then some vision which she had since gained—gained through Monte. It was that which made her understand Peter now, and the wonder of his love and the glory and sacredness of all love. It was that which made her understand herself now.

She got to her feet, staring into the dark toward the seashore.

"Monte, forgive me—forgive me!" she choked.

She had trifled with the biggest thing in his life and in her life. She shouldered the full blame. Monte knew nothing either of himself or of her. He was just Monte, honest and four-square, living up to his bargain. But she had seen the light in his eyes—the eyes that should have led him to the Holy Grail. He would have had to go such a little way—only as far as her outstretched arms.

She shrank back from the window, her head bowed. It had been her privilege as a woman to be wiser than he. She should have known! Now—the thought wrenched like a physical pain—there was nothing left to her but renunciation. She must help him to be free. She must force him free. She owed that to him and to herself. It was only so that she might ever feel clean again.

Moaning his name, she flung herself upon the bed. So she lay until summoned back to life by Marie, who brought her the card of Miss Beatrice Noyes.

Marjory took the time to bathe her dry cheeks in hot water and to do over her hair before admitting the girl; but, even with those precautions, Beatrice paused at the entrance as if startled by her appearance.

"Perhaps you do not feel like seeing any one to-night," she suggested.

"I do want to see you," answered Marjory. "I want to hear about Peter. But my head—would you mind if we sat in the dark?"

"I think that would be better—if we are to talk about Peter."

The phrase puzzled Marjory, but she turned out the lights and placed two chairs near the open windows.

"Now tell me from the beginning," she requested.

"The beginning came soon after you went away," replied Beatrice in a low voice.

Marjory leaned back wearily. If there were to be more complications for which she must hold herself accountable, she felt that she could not listen. Surely she had lived through enough for one day.

"Peter cared a great deal for you," Beatrice faltered on.

"Why?"

It was a cry in the night.

Impulsively the younger girl leaned forward and fumbled for her hands.

"You did n't realize it?" she asked hopefully.

"I realized nothing then. I realized nothing yesterday," cried Marjory. "It is only to-day that I began to realize anything."

"To-day?"

"Only to-night."

"It was the sight of Peter looking so unlike himself that opened your heart," nodded Beatrice.

"Not my heart—just my eyes," returned Marjory.

"Your heart too," insisted Beatrice; "for it's only through your heart that you can open Peter's eyes."

"I—I don't understand."

"Because he loves you," breathed Beatrice.

"BECAUSE HE LOVES YOU," BREATHED BEATRICE

"Because he loves you," breathed Beatrice.

"No. No—not that."

"You don't know how much," went on the girl excitedly. "None of us knew how much—until after you went. Oh, he'd never forgive me if he knew I was talking like this! But I can't help it. It was because he would not talk—because he kept it a secret all to himself that this came upon him. They told me at the hospital that it was overwork and worry, and that he had only one chance in a hundred. But I sat by his side, Marjory, night and day, and coaxed him back. Little by little he grew stronger—all except his poor eyes. It was then he told me the truth: how he had tried to forget you in his work."

"He—he blamed me?"

Beatrice was still clinging to her hands.

"No," she answered quickly. "He did not blame you. We never blame those we love, do we?"

"But we hurt those we love!"

"Only when we don't understand. You did not know he loved you like that, did you?"

Marjory withdrew her hands.

"He had no right!" she cried.

Beatrice was silent a moment. There was a great deal here that she herself did not understand. But, though she herself had never loved, there was a great deal she did understand. She spoke as if thinking aloud.

"I have not found love—yet," she said. "But I never thought it was a question of right when people loved. I thought it—it just happened."

Marjory drew a quick breath.

"Yes; it is like that," she admitted.

Only, she was not thinking of Peter. She was thinking of herself. A week ago she would have smiled at that phrase. Even yesterday she would have smiled a little. Love was something a woman or man undertook or not at will. It was a condition to choose as one chose one's style of living. It was accepted or rejected, as suited one's pleasure. If a woman preferred her freedom, then that was her right.

Then, less than an hour ago, she had flung out her hands toward the shadowy figure of a man walking alone by the sea, her heart aching with a great need for the love that might have been hers had she not smiled. That need, springing of her own love, had just happened. The fulfillment of it was a matter to be decided by her own conscience; but the love itself had involved no question of right. She felt a wave of sympathy for Peter. She was able to feel for him now as never before. Poor Peter, lying there alone in the hospital! How the ache, unsatisfied, ate into one.

"Peter would n't tell me at first," Beatrice was running on. "His lips were as tight closed as his poor bandaged eyes."

"The blindness," broke in Marjory. "That is not permanent?"

"I will tell you what the doctor told me," Beatrice replied slowly. "He said that, while his eyes were badly overstrained, the seat of the trouble was mental. 'He is worrying,' he told me. 'Remove the cause of that and he has a chance.'"

"So you have come to me for that?"

"It seems like fate," said Peter's sister, with something of awe in her voice. "When, little by little, Peter told me of his love, I thought of only one thing: of finding you. I wanted to cable you, because I—I thought you would come if you knew. But Peter would not allow that. He made me promise not to do that. Then, as he grew stronger, and the doctor told us that perhaps an ocean voyage would help him, I wanted to bring him to you. He would not allow that either. He thought you were in Paris, and insisted that we take the Mediterranean route. Then—we happen upon you outside the hotel we chose by chance! Does n't it seem as if back of such a thing as that there must be something we don't understand; something higher than just what we may think right or wrong?"

"No, no; that's impossible," exclaimed Marjory.

"Why?"

"Because then we'd have to believe everything that happened was right. And it is n't."

"Was our coming here not right?"

Marjory did not answer.

"If you could have seen the hope in Peter's face when I left him!"

"He does n't know!" choked Marjory.

"He knows you are here, and that is all he needs to know," answered Beatrice.

"If it were only as simple as that."

The younger girl rose and, moving to the other's side, placed an arm over the drooping shoulders.

"Marjory dear," she said. "I feel to-night more like Peter than myself. I have listened so many hours in the dark as he talked about you. He—he has given me a new idea of love. I'd always thought of love in a—a sort of fairy-book way. I did n't think of it as having much to do with everyday life. I supposed that some time a knight would come along on horseback—if ever he came—and take me off on a long holiday."

Marjory gave a start. The girl was smoothing her hair.

"It would always be May-time," she went on, "and we'd have nothing to do but gather posies in the sunshine. We'd laugh and sing, and there'd be no care and no worries. Did you ever think of love that way?"

"Yes."

The girl spoke more slowly now, as if anxious to be quite accurate:—

"But Peter seemed to think of other things. When we talked of you it was as if he wanted you to be a part of himself and help with the big things he was planning to do. He had so many wonderful plans in which you were to help. Instead of running away from cares and worries, it was as though meeting these was what was going to make it May-time. Instead of riding off to some fairy kingdom, he seemed to feel that it was this that would make a fairy kingdom even of New York. Because"—she lowered her voice—"it was of a home and of children he talked, and of what a fine mother you would make. He talked of that—and somehow, Marjory, it made me proud just to be a woman! Oh, perhaps I should n't repeat such things!"

Marjory sprang to her feet.

"You should n't repeat them!" she exclaimed. "You mustn't repeat anything more! And I must n't listen!"

"It is only because you're the woman I came to know so well, sitting by his bed in the dark, that I dared," she said gently.

"You'll go now?" pleaded Marjory. "I must n't listen to any more."

Silently, as if frightened by what she had already said, Beatrice moved toward the door.

Marjory hurried after her.

"You're good," she cried, "and Peter's good! And I—"

The girl finished for her:—

"No matter what happens, you'll always be to me Peter's Marjory," she said. "You'll always keep me proud."

CHAPTER XVI
A WALK ON THE QUAY

Monte, stepping out of his room early after a restless night, saw a black-haired young man wearing a shade over his eyes fumbling about for the elevator button. He had the thin, nervous mouth and the square jaw of an American.

Monte stepped up to him.

"May I help you?" he asked.

"Thank you," answered Noyes; "I thought I could make it alone, but there is n't much light here."

Monte took his arm and assisted him to the elevator. The man appeared half blind. His heart went out to him at once. As they reached the first floor the stranger again hesitated. He smiled nervously.

"I wanted to get out in the air," he explained. "I thought I could find a valet to accompany me."

Monte hesitated. He did not want to intrude, but there was something about this helpless American that appealed to him. Impulsively he said: "Would you come with me? Covington is my name. I 'm just off for a walk along the quay."

"Noyes is my name," answered Peter. "I'd like to come, but I don't want to trouble you to that extent."

Monte took his arm.

"Come on," he said. "It's a bully morning."

"The air smells good," nodded Noyes. "I should have waited for my sister, but I was a bit restless. Do you mind asking the clerk to let her know where I am when she comes down?"

Monte called Henri.

"Inform Miss Noyes we'll be on the quay," he told him.

They walked in silence until they reached the boulevard bordering the ocean.

"We have the place to ourselves," said Monte. "If I walk too fast for you, let me know."

"I 'm not very sure of my feet yet," apologized Noyes. "I suppose in time I'll get used to this."

"Good Lord, you don't expect it to last?"

"No. They tell me I have a fighting chance."

"How did it happen?"

"Used them a bit too much, I guess," answered Noyes.

"That's tough."

"A man has so darned much to do and such a little while to do it in," exclaimed Noyes.

"You must live in New York."

"Yes. And you?"

"I generally drift back for the holidays. I've been traveling a good deal for the last ten years."

"I see. Some sort of research work?"

The way Noyes used that word "work" made Monte uncomfortable. It was as if he took it for granted that a man who was a man must have a definite occupation.

"I don't know that you would call it exactly that," answered Monte. "I've just been knocking around. I have n't had anything in particular to do. What are you in?"

"Law. I wonder if you're Harvard?"

"Sure thing. And you?"

Noyes named his class—a class six years later than Monte's.

"Well, we have something in common there, anyhow," said Covington cordially. "My father was Harvard Law School. He practiced in Philadelphia."

"I've always lived in New York. I was born there, and I love it. I like the way it makes you hustle—the challenge to get in and live—"

He stopped abruptly, putting one hand to his eyes.

"They hurt?" asked Monte anxiously.

"You need your eyes in New York," he answered simply.

"You went in too hard," suggested Monte.

"Is there any other way?" cried Noyes.

"I used to play football a little," said Monte. "I suppose it's something like that—when a man gets the spirit of the thing. When you hit the line you want to feel that you 're putting into it every ounce in you."

Noyes nodded.

"Into your work—into your life."

"Into your life?" queried Monte.

"Into everything."

Monte turned to look at the man. His thin lips had come together in a straight line. His hollow cheeks were flushed. Every sense was as alert as a fencer's. If he had lived long like that, no wonder his eyes had gone bad. Yet last night Monte himself had lived like that, pacing his room hour after hour. Only it was not work that had given a cutting edge to each minute—not life, whatever Noyes meant by that. His thoughts had all been of a woman. Was that life? Was it what Noyes had meant when he said "everything"?

"This bucking the line all the time raises the devil with you," he said.

"How?" demanded Noyes.

The answer Monte could have returned was obvious. The fact that amazed him was that Noyes could have asked the question with the sun and the blue sky shut away from him. It only proved again what Monte had always maintained—that excesses of any kind, whether of rum or ambition or—or love—drove men stark mad. Blind as a bat from overwork, Noyes still asked the question.

"Look here," said Monte, with a frown. "Before the big events the coach used to take us one side and make us believe that the one thing in life we wanted was that game. He used to make us as hungry for it as a starved dog for a bone. He used to make us ache for it. So we used to wade in and tear ourselves all to pieces to get it."

"Well?"

"If we won it was n't so much; if we lost—it left us aching worse than before."

"Yes."

"There was the crowd that sat and watched us. They did n't care the way we cared. We went back to the locker building in strings; they went off to a comfortable dinner."

"And the moral?" demanded Noyes.

"Is not to care too darned much, is n't it?" growled Monte.

"If you want a comfortable dinner," nodded Noyes.

"Or a comfortable night's sleep. Or if you want to wake up in the morning with the world looking right."

Again Monte saw the impulsive movement of the man's hand to his eyes.

He said quickly: "I did n't mean to refer to that."

"I forget it for a while. Then—suddenly—I remember it."

"You wanted something too hard," said Monte gently.

"I wanted something with all there was in me. I still want it."

"You're not sorry, then?"

"If I were sorry for that, I'd be sorry I was alive."

"But the cost!"

"Of what value is a thing that doesn't cost?" returned Noyes. "All the big things cost big. Half the joy in them is pitting yourself against that and paying the price. The ache you speak of—that's credited to the joy in the end. Those men in the grand-stand don't know that. If you fight hard, you can't lose, no matter what the score is against you."

"You mean it's possible to get some of your fun out of the game itself?"

"What else is there to life—if you pick the things worth fighting for?"

"Then, if you lose—"

"You've lived," concluded Noyes.

"It's men like you who ought really to win," exclaimed Monte. "I hope you get what you went after."

"I mean to," answered Noyes, with grim determination.

They had turned and were coming back in the direction of the hotel when Monte saw a girlish figure hurrying toward them.

"I think your sister is coming," said Monte.

"Then you can be relieved of me," answered Noyes.

"But I 've enjoyed this walk immensely. I hope we can take another. Are you here for long?"

"Indefinitely. And you?"

"Also indefinitely."

Miss Noyes was by their side now.

"Sister—this is Mr. Covington," Peter introduced her.

Miss Noyes smiled.

"I've good news for you, Peter," she said. "I've just heard from Marjory, and she'll see you at ten."

Monte was startled by the name, but was even more startled by the look of joy that illuminated the features of the man by his side. For a second it was as if his blind eyes had suddenly come to life.

Monte caught his breath.

CHAPTER XVII
JUST MONTE

Monte was at the Hôtel d'Angleterre at nine. In response to his card he received a brief note.

Dear Monte [he read]: Please don't ask to see me this morning. I'm so mixed up I'm afraid I won't be at all good company.

Yours, MARJORY.

Monte sent back this note in reply:—

Dear Marjory: If you're mixed up, I'm just the one you ought to see. You've been thinking again.

MONTE.

She came into the office looking like a hunted thing; but he stepped forward to meet her with a boyish good humor that reassured her in an instant. The firm grip of his hand alone was enough to steady her. Her tired eyes smiled gratitude.

"I never expected to be married and deserted—all in one week," he said lightly. "What's the trouble?"

He felt like a comedian trying to be funny with the heart gone out of him. But he knew she expected no less. He must remain just Monte or he would only frighten her the more. No matter if his heart pounded until he could not catch his breath, he must play the care-free chump of a *compagnon de voyage*. That was all she had married—all she wanted. She glanced at his arm in its black sling.

"Who tied that this morning?" she asked.

"The valet."

"He did n't do it at all nicely. There's a little sun parlor on the next floor. Come with me and I 'll do it over."

He followed her upstairs and into a room filled with flowers and wicker chairs. She stood before him and readjusted the handkerchief, so near that he thought he felt her breath. It was a test for a man, and he came through it nobly.

"There—that's better," she said. "Now take the big chair in the sun."

She drew it forward a little, though he protested at so much attention. She dropped into another seat a little away from him.

"Well?" he inquired. "Aren't you going to tell me about it?"

He was making it as easy as possible—easier than she had anticipated.

"Won't you please smoke?"

He lighted a cigarette.

"Now we're off," he encouraged her.

He was leaning back with one leg crossed over the other—a big, wholesome boy. His blue eyes this morning were the color of the sky, and just as clean and just as untroubled. As she studied him the thought uppermost in her mind was that she must not hurt him. She must be very careful about that. She must give him nothing to worry over.

"Monte," she began, "I guess women have a lot of queer notions men don't know anything about. Can't we let it go at that?"

"If you wish," he nodded. "Only—are you going to stay here?"

"For a little while, anyway," she answered.

"You mean—a day or two?"

"Or a week or two."

"You'd rather not tell me why?"

"If you please—not," she answered quickly.

He thought a moment, and then asked:—

"It was n't anything I did?"

"No, no," she assured him. "You've been so good, Monte."

He was so good with her now—so gentle and considerate. It made her heart ache. With her chin in hand, elbow upon the arm of her chair, she was apparently looking at him more or less indifferently, when what she would have liked to do was to smooth away the perplexed frown between his brows.

"Then," he asked, "your coming here has n't anything to do with me?"

She could not answer that directly. With her cheeks burning and her lips dry, she tried to think just what to say. Above all things, she must not worry him!

"It has to do with you and myself and—Peter Noyes," she answered.

"Peter Noyes!"

He sat upright.

"He is at the Hôtel des Roses—with his sister," Marjory ran on hurriedly. "They are both old friends, and I met them quite by accident last night. Suddenly, Monte,—they made my position there impossible. They gave me a new point of view on myself—on you. I guess it was an American point of view. What had seemed right before did not seem right then."

"Is that why you resumed your maiden name?"

"That is why. But sooner or later Peter will know the truth, won't he?"

"How will he know?"

"The name you signed on the register."

"That's so, too," Monte admitted. "But that says only 'Madame Covington.' Madame Covington might be any one."

He smiled, but his lips were tense.

"She may have been called home unexpectedly."

The girl hid her face in her hands. He rose and stepped to her side.

"There, there," he said gently. "Don't worry about that. There is no reason why they should ever associate you with her. If they make any inquiries of me about madame, I'll just say she has gone away for a little while—perhaps for a week or two. Is that right?"

"I—I don't know."

"Nothing unusual about that. Wives are always going away. Even Chic's wife goes away every now and then. As for you, little woman, I think you did the only thing possible. I met that Peter Noyes this morning."

Startled, she raised her face from her hands.

"You met—Peter Noyes?" she asked slowly.

"Quite by chance. He was on his way to walk, and I took him with me. He's a wonderful fellow, Marjory."

"You talked with him?"

He nodded.

"He takes life mighty seriously."

"Too seriously, Monte," she returned.

"It's what made him blind; and yet—there's something worth while about a man who gets into the game that way. Hanged if he did n't leave me feeling uncomfortable."

She looked worried.

"How, Monte?"

"Oh, as though I ought to be doing something instead of just kicking around the Continent. Do you know I had a notion of studying law at one time?"

"But there was no need of it, was there?"

"Not in one way. Only, I suppose I could have made myself useful somewhere, even if I did n't have to earn a living. Maybe there's a use for every one—somewhere."

He had left her side, and was staring out the window toward the ocean. She watched him anxiously. She had never seen him like this, and yet, in a way, this was the same Monte in whose eyes she had caught a glimpse of the wonderful bright light. It was the man who had leaned toward her as they walked on the shore the night before they reached Nice—a gallant prince of the fairy-books, ready to step into real life and be a gallant prince there.

Monte had never had a chance. Had he been left as Peter Noyes had been left, dependent upon himself, he would have done all that Peter had done, without losing his smile. Marjory must not allow him to lose that now. His mouth was drooping with such exaggerated melancholy that she felt something must be done at once. She began to laugh. He turned quickly.

"You look as if you had lost your last friend," she chided him. "If talking with Peter Noyes does that to you, I don't think you had better talk with him any more."

"He's worth more to-day, blind, than I with my two eyes."

"The trouble with Peter is that he can't smile," she answered. "After all, it would be a sad world if no one were left to smile."

The words brought back to him the phrase she had used at the Normandie: "I am depending on you to keep me normal."

Here was something right at hand for him to do, and a man's job at that. He had wanted a chance to play the game, and here it was. Perhaps the game was not so big as some,—it concerned only her and him,—but there was a certain added challenge in playing the little game hard. Besides, the importance of the game was a good deal in the point of view. If, for him, it was big, that was enough.

As he stood before her now, the demand upon him for all his nerve was enough to satisfy any man. To assume before her the pose of the carefree chump that she needed to balance her own nervous fears—to do this with every muscle in him straining toward her, with the beauty of her making him dizzy, with hot words leaping for expression to his dry lips, those facts, after all, made the game seem not so small.

"Where are you going to lunch to-day?" he asked.

"I don't know, Monte," she answered indifferently. "I told Peter he could come over at ten."

"I see. Want to lunch with him?"

"I don't want to lunch with any one."

"He'll probably expect you. I was going to look at some villas to-day; but I suppose that's all off."

Her cheeks turned scarlet.

"Yes."

"Then I guess I'll walk to Monte Carlo and lunch there. How about dinner?"

"If they see us together—"

"Ask them to come along too. You can tell them I'm an old friend. I am that, am I not?"

"One of the oldest and best," she answered earnestly.

"Then I'll call you up when I come back. Good luck."

With a nod and a smile, he left her.

From the window she watched him out of sight. He did not turn. There was no reason in the world why she should have expected him to turn. He had a pleasant day before him. He would amuse himself at the Casino, enjoy a good luncheon, smoke a cigarette in the sunshine, and call her up at his leisure when he returned. Except for the light obligation of ascertaining her wishes concerning dinner, it was the routine he had followed for ten years. It had kept him satisfied, kept him content. Doubtless, if he were left undisturbed, it would keep him satisfied and content for another decade. He would always be able to walk away from her without turning back.

CHAPTER XVIII
PETER

Beatrice brought Peter at ten, and, in spite of the mute appeal of Marjory's eyes, stole off on tiptoe and left her alone with him.

"Has Trix gone?" demanded Peter.

"Yes."

"She shouldn't have done that," he complained.

Marjory made him comfortable in the chair Monte had lately occupied, finding a cushion for his head.

"Please don't do those things," he objected. "You make me feel as if I were wearing a sign begging for pity."

"How can any one help pitying you, when they see you like this, Peter?" she asked gently.

"What right have they to do it?" he demanded.

"Right?"

She frowned at that word. So many things in her life seemed to have been decided without respect for right.

"I'm the only one to say whether I shall be pitied or not," he declared. "I've lost the use of my eyes temporarily by my own fault. I don't like it; but I refuse to be pitied."

Marjory was surprised to find him so aggressive. It was not what she expected after listening to Beatrice. It changed her whole attitude toward him instantly from one of guarded condolence to honest admiration. There was no whine here. He was blaming no one—neither himself nor her. It was with a wave of deep and sincere sympathy, springing spontaneously from within herself, that she spoke.

"Peter," she said, "I won't pity you any more. But if I 'm sorry for you—awfully sorry—you won't mind that?"

"I'd rather you would n't think of my eyes at all," he answered unsteadily. "I can almost forget them myself—with you."

"Then," she said, "we'll forget them. Are you going to stay here long, Peter?"

"Are you?"

"My plans are uncertain. I don't think I shall ever make any more plans."

"You must n't let yourself feel that way," Peter returned. "The thing to do, if one scheme fails, is to start another—right off."

"But nothing ever comes out as you expect."

"That gives you a chance to try again."

"You can't keep that up forever?"

"Forever and ever," he nodded. "It's what makes life worth living."

"Peter," she said below her breath, "you're wonderful."

He seemed to clear the muggy air around her like a summer shower. In touch with his fine courage, her own returned. She felt herself steadier and calmer than she had been for a week.

"What if you make mistakes, Peter?"

"It's the only way you learn," he answered. "There's a new note in your voice, Marjory. Have—you been learning?"

His meaning was clear. He leaned forward as if trying to pierce the darkness between them. His thin white hands were tight upon the chair arms.

"At least, I've been making mistakes," she answered uneasily.

She felt, for a second, as if she could pour out her troubles to him—as if he would listen patiently and give her of his wisdom and strength. It would be easier—she was ashamed of the thought, but it held true—because he could not see. Almost—she could tell him of herself and of Monte.

"There's such a beautiful woman in you!" he explained passionately.

With her heart beating fast, she dropped back in her chair. There was the old ring in his voice—the old masterful decision that used to frighten her. There used to be moments when she was afraid that he might command her to come with him as with authority, and that she would go.

"I 've always known that you'd learn some day all the fine things that are in you—all the fine things that lay ahead of you to do as a woman," he ran on. "You've only been waiting; that's all."

He could not see her cheeks—she was thankful for that. But the wonder was that he did not hear the pounding of her heart. He spoke like this, not knowing of this last week.

"You remember all the things I said to you—before you left?"

"Yes."

"I can't say them to you now. I must wait until I get my eyes back. Then I shall say them again, and perhaps—"

"Do you think I 'd let you wait for your eyes?" she cried.

"You mean that now—"

"No, no, Peter," she interrupted, in a panic. "I did n't mean I could listen now. Only I did n't want you to think I was so selfish that if it were possible to share the light with you I—I would n't share the dark too."

"There would n't be any dark for me at all if you shared it," he answered gently.

Then she saw his lips tighten.

"We must n't talk of that," he said. "We must n't think of it."

Yet, of all the many things they discussed this morning, nothing left Marjory more to think about. It seemed that, so far, her freedom had done nothing but harm. She had intended no harm. She had desired only to lead her own life day by day, quite by herself. So she had fled from Peter—with this result; then she had fled from Teddy, who had lost his head completely; finally she had fled, not from Monte but with him, because that seemed quite the safest thing to do. It had proved the most dangerous of all! If she had driven Peter blind, Monte—if he only knew it—had brought him sweet revenge, because he had made her, not blind, but something that was worse, a thousand times worse!

There was some hope for Peter. It is so much easier to cure blindness than vision. Always she must see the light that had leaped to Monte's eyes, kindled from the fire in her own soul. Always she must see him coming to her outstretched arms, knowing that she had lost the right to lift her arms. Perhaps she must even see him going to other arms, that flame born of her breathed into fuller life by other lips. If not—then the ultimate curse of watching him remain just Monte, knowing he might have been so much more. This because she had dared trifle with that holy passion and so had made herself unworthy of it.

Peter was telling her of his work; of what he had accomplished already and of what he hoped to accomplish. She heard him as from a distance, and answered mechanically his questions, while she pursued her own thoughts.

It seemed almost as if a woman was not allowed to remain negative; that either she must accomplish positive good or positive harm. So far, she had accomplished only harm; and now here was an opportunity that was almost an obligation to offset that to some degree. She must free Monte as soon as possible. That was necessary in any event. She owed it to him. It was a sacred obligation that she must pay to save even the frayed remnant of her pride. This had nothing to do with Peter. She saw now it would have been necessary just the same, even if Peter had not come to make it clearer. Until she gave up the name to which she had no right, with which she had so shamelessly trifled, she must feel only glad that Peter could not see into her eyes.

So Monte would go on his way again, and she would be left—she and Peter. If, then, what Beatrice said was true,—if it was within her power, at no matter what sacrifice, to give Peter back the sight she had taken,—then so she might undo some of the wrong she had done. The bigger the sacrifice, the fiercer the fire might rage to burn her clean. Because she had thought to sacrifice nothing, she had been forced to sacrifice everything; if now she sacrificed everything, perhaps she could get back a little peace in return. She would give her life to Peter—give him everything that was left in her to give. Humbly she would serve him and nurse the light back into his eyes. Was it possible to do this?

She saw Beatrice at the door, and rose to meet her.

"You're to lunch with me," she said. "Then, for dinner, Mr. Covington has asked us all to join him."

"Covington?" exclaimed Peter. "Is n't he the man who was so decent to me this morning?"

"He said he met you," answered Marjory.

"I liked him," declared Peter. "I'll be mighty glad to see more of him."

"And I too," nodded Beatrice. "He looked so very romantic with his injured arm."

"Monte romantic?" smiled Marjory. "That's the one thing in the world he is n't."

"Just who is he, anyway?" inquired Beatrice.

"He's just Monte," answered Marjory.

"And Madame Monte—where is she? I noticed by the register there is such a person."

"I—I think he said she had been called away—unexpectedly," Marjory gasped.

She turned aside with an uncomfortable feeling that Beatrice had noticed her confusion.

CHAPTER XIX
AN EXPLANATION

The following week Monte devoted himself wholly to the entertainment of Marjory and her friends. He placed his car at their disposal, and planned for them daily trips with the thoroughness of a courier, though he generally found some excuse for not going himself. His object was simple: to keep Marjory's days so filled that she would have no time left in which to worry. He wanted to help her, as far as possible, to forget the preceding week, which had so disturbed her. To this end nothing could be better for her than Peter and Beatrice Noyes, who were so simply and honestly plain, everyday Americans. They were just the wholesome, good-natured companions she needed to offset the morbid frame of mind into which he had driven her. Especially Peter. He was good for her and she was good for him.

The more he talked with Peter Noyes the better he liked him. At the end of the day—after seeing them started in the morning, Monte used to go out and walk his legs off till dinner-time—he enjoyed dropping into a chair by the side of Peter. It was wonderful how already Peter had picked up. He had gained not only in weight and color, but a marked mental change was noticeable. He always came back from his ride in high spirits. So completely did he ignore his blindness that Monte, talking with him in the dark, found himself forgetting it—awakening to the fact each time with a shock when it was necessary to offer an assisting arm.

It was the man's enthusiasm Monte admired. He seemed to be always alert—always keen. Yet, as near as he could find out, his life had been anything but adventuresome or varied. After leaving the law school he had settled down in a New York office and just plugged along. He confessed that this was the first vacation he had taken since he began practice.

"You can hardly call this a vacation!" exclaimed Monte.

"Man dear," answered Peter earnestly, "you don't know what these days mean to me."

"You sure are entitled to all the fun you can get out of them," returned Monte. "But I hate to think how I'd feel under the same circumstances."

"I don't believe there is much difference between men," answered Peter. "I imagine that about certain things we all feel a good deal alike."

"I wonder," mused Monte. "I can't imagine myself, for instance, living twelve months in the year in New York and being enthusiastic about it."

"What do you do when you're there?" inquired Peter.

"Not much of anything," admitted Monte.

"Then you're no more in New York when you're there than in Jericho," answered Peter. "You 've got to get into the game really to live in New York. You 've got to work and be one of the million others before you can get the feel of the city. Best of all, a man ought to marry there. You're married, are n't you, Covington?"

"Eh?"

"Did n't Beatrice tell me you registered here with your wife?"

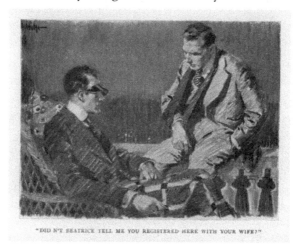

"DID N'T BEATRICE TELL ME YOU REGISTERED HERE WITH YOUR WIFE?"

"Did n't Beatrice tell me you registered here with your wife?"

Monte moistened his lips.

"Yes—she was here for a day. She—she was called away."

"That's too bad. I hope we'll have an opportunity to meet her before we leave."

"Thanks."

"She ought to help you understand New York."

"Perhaps she would. We've never been there together."

"Been married long?"

"No."

"So you have n't any children."

"Hardly."

"Then," said Peter, "you have your whole life ahead of you. You have n't begun to live anywhere yet."

"And you?"

"It's the same with me," confessed Peter, with a quick breath. "Only—well, I haven't been able to make even the beginning you 've made."

Monte leaned forward with quickened interest.

"That's the thing you wanted so hard?" he asked.

"Yes."

"To marry and have children?"

Monte was silent a moment, and then he added:—

"I know a man who did that."

"A man who does n't is n't a man, is he?"

"I—I don't know," confessed Monte. "I 've visited this friend once or twice. Did you ever see a kiddy with the croup?"

"No," admitted Peter.

"You're darned lucky. It's just as though—as though some one had the little devil by the throat, trying to strangle him."

"There are things you can do."

"Things you can try to do. But mostly you stand around with your hands tied, waiting to see what's going to happen."

"Well?" queried Peter, evidently puzzled.

"That's only one of a thousand things that can happen to 'em. There are worse things. They are happening every day."

"Well?"

"When I think of Chic and his children I think of him pacing the hall with his forehead all sweaty with the ache inside of him. Nothing pleasant about that, is there?"

Peter did not answer for a moment, and then what he said seemed rather pointless.

"What of it?" he asked.

"Only this," answered Monte uneasily. "When you speak of a wife and children you have to remember those facts. You have to consider that you're going to be torn all to shoe-strings every so often. Maybe you open the gates of heaven, but you throw open the gates of hell too. There's no more jogging along in between on the good old earth."

"Good Lord!" exclaimed Peter. "You consider such things?"

"I've always tried to stay normal," answered Monte uneasily.

"Yet you said you're married?"

"Even so, is n't it possible for a man to keep his head?" demanded Monte.

"I don't understand," replied Peter.

"Look here—I don't want to intrude in your affairs, but I don't suppose you are talking merely abstractedly. You have some one definite in mind?"

"Yes."

"Then you ought to understand; you've kept steady."

"I wouldn't be like this if I had," answered Peter.

"You mean your eyes."

"I tried to forget her because she wasn't ready to listen. I turned to my work, and put in twenty hours a day. It was a fool thing to do. And yet—"

Monte held his breath.

"From the depths I saw the heights, I saw the wonderful beauty of the peaks."

"And still see them?"

"Clearer than ever now."

"Then you aren't sorry she came into your life?"

"Sorry, man?" exclaimed Peter. "Even at this price—even if there were no hope ahead, I'd still have my visions."

"But there is hope?"

"I have one chance in a thousand. It's more than anything I 've had up to now."

"One in a thousand is a fighting chance," Monte returned.

"You speak as if that were more than you had."

"It was."

"Yet you won out."

"How?" demanded Monte.

"She married you."

"Yes," answered Monte, "that's true. I say, old man—it's getting a bit cool here. Perhaps we'd better go in."

Monte had planned for them a drive to Cannes the day Beatrice sent word to Marjory that she would be unable to go.

"But you two will go, won't you?" she concluded her note. "Peter will be terribly disappointed if you don't."

So they went, leaving at ten o'clock. At ten-fifteen Beatrice came downstairs, and ran into Monte just as he was about to start his walk.

"You're feeling better?" he asked politely.

She shook her head.

"I—I'm afraid I told a fib."

"You mean you stayed because you did n't want to go."

"Yes. But I did n't say I had a headache."

"I know how you feel about that," he returned. "Leaving people to guess wrong lets you out in one way, and in another it does n't."

She appeared surprised at his directness. She had expected him to pass the incident over lightly.

"It was for Peter's sake, anyhow," she tried to justify her position. "But don't let me delay you, please. I know you 're off for your morning walk."

That was true. But he was interested in that statement she had just made that it was for Peter's sake she had remained behind. It revealed an amazingly dense ignorance of both her brother's position and Marjory's. On no other theory could he make it seem consistent for her to encourage a tête-à-tête between a married woman and a man as deeply in love with some one else as Peter was.

"Won't you come along a little way?" he asked. "We can turn back at any time."

She hesitated a moment—but only a moment.

"Thanks."

She fell into step at his side as he sought the quay.

"You've been very good to Peter," she said. "I've wanted a chance to tell you so."

"You did n't remain behind for that, I hope," he smiled.

"No," she admitted; "but I do appreciate your kindness. Peter has had such a terrible time of it."

"And yet," mused Monte aloud, "he does n't seem to feel that way himself."

"He has confided in you?"

"A little. He told me he regretted nothing."

"He has such fine courage!" she exclaimed.

"Not that alone. He has had some beautiful dreams."

"That's because of his courage."

"It takes courage, then, to dream?" Monte asked.

"Don't you think it does—with your eyes gone?"

"With or without eyes," he admitted.

"You don't know what he's been through," she frowned. "Even he does n't know. When I came to him, there was so little of him left. I 'll never forget the first sight I had of him in the hospital. Thin and white and blind, he lay there as though dead."

He looked at the frail young woman by his side. She must have had fine courage too. There was something of Peter in her.

"And you nursed him back."

She blushed at the praise.

"Perhaps I helped a little; but, after all, it was the dreams he had that counted most. All I did was to listen and try to make them real to him. I tried to make him hope."

"That was fine."

"He loved so hard, with all there was in him, as he does everything," she explained.

"I suppose that was the trouble," he nodded.

She turned quickly. It was as if he said that was the mistake.

"After all, that's just love, is n't it? There can't be any halfway about it, can there?"

"I wonder."

"You—you wonder, Mr. Covington?"

He was stupid at first. He did not get the connection. Then, as she turned her dark eyes full upon him, the blood leaped to his cheeks. He was married—that was what she was trying to tell him. He had a wife, and so presumably knew what love was. For her to assume anything else, for him to admit anything else, was impossible.

"Perhaps we'd better turn back," she said uneasily.

He felt like a cad. He turned instantly.

"I'm afraid I did n't make myself very clear," he faltered. "We are n't all of us like Peter."

"There is no one in the world quite as good as Peter," the girl declared.

"Then you should n't blame me too much," he suggested.

"It is not for me to criticize you at all," she returned somewhat stiffly.

"But you did."

"How?"

"When you suggested turning back. It was as if you had determined I was not quite a proper person to walk with."

"Mr. Covington!" she protested.

"We may as well be frank. It seems to be a misfortune of mine lately to get things mixed up. Peter is helping me to see straight. That's why I like to talk with him."

"He sees so straight himself."

"That's it."

"If only now he recovers his eyes."

"He says there's hope."

"It all depends upon her," she said.

"Upon this woman?"

"Upon this one woman."

"If she realized it—"

"She does," broke in Beatrice. "I made her realize it. I went to her and told her."

"You did that?"

She raised her head in swift challenge.

"Even though Peter commanded me not to—even though I knew he would never forgive me if he learned."

"You women are so wonderful," breathed Monte.

"With Peter's future—with his life at stake—what else could I do?"

"And she, knowing that, refused to come to him?"

"Fate brought us to her."

"Then," exclaimed Monte, "what are you doing here?"

She stopped and faced him. It was evident that he was sincere.

"You men—all men are so stupid at times!" she cried, with a little laugh.

He shook his head slowly.

"I 'll have to admit it."

"Why, he's with her now," she laughed. "That's why I stayed at home to-day."

Monte held his breath for a second, and then he said:—

"You mean, the woman Peter loves is—is Marjory Stockton?"

"No other. I thought he must have told you. If not, I thought you must have guessed it from her."

"Why, no," he admitted; "I did n't."

"Then you've had your eyes closed."

"That's it," he nodded; "I've had my eyes closed. Why, that explains a lot of things."

Impulsively the girl placed her hand on Monte's arm.

"As an old friend of hers, you'll use your influence to help Peter?"

"I 'll do what I can."

"Then I'm so glad I told you."

"Yes," agreed Monte. "I suppose it is just as well for me to know."

CHAPTER XX
PAYING LIKE A MAN

Everything considered, Monte should have been glad at the revelation Beatrice made to him. If Peter were in love with Marjory and she with Peter—why, it solved his own problem, by the simple process of elimination, neatly and with despatch. All that remained for him to do was to remove himself from the awkward triangle as soon as possible. He must leave Marjory free, and Peter would look after the rest. No doubt a divorce on the grounds of desertion could be easily arranged; and thus, by that one stroke, they two would be made happy, and he—well, what the devil was to become of him?

The answer was obvious. It did not matter a picayune to any one what became of him. What had he ever done to make his life worth while to any one? He had never done any particular harm, that was true; but neither had he done any particular good. It is the positive things that count, when a man stands before the judgment-seat; and that is where Monte stood on the night Marjory came back from Cannes by the side of Peter, with her eyes sparkling and her cheeks flushed as if she had come straight from Eden.

They all dined together, and Monte grubbed hungrily for every look she vouchsafed him, for every word she tossed him. She had been more than ordinarily vivacious, spurred on partly by Beatrice and partly by Peter. Monte had felt himself merely an onlooker. That, in fact, was all he was. That was all he had been his whole life.

He dodged Peter this evening to escape their usual after-dinner talk, and went to his room. He was there now, with his face white and tense.

He had been densely stupid from the first, as Beatrice had informed him. Any man of the world ought to have suspected something when, at the first sight of Peter, she ran away. She had never run from him. Women run only when there is danger of capture, and she had nothing to fear from him in that way. She was safe with him. She dared even come with him to escape those from whom there might be some possible danger. Until now he had been rather proud of this—as if it were some honor. She had trusted him as she would not trust other men. It had made him throw back his shoulders—dense fool that he was!

She had trusted him because she did not fear him; she did not fear him because there was nothing in him to fear. It was not that he was more decent than other men: it was merely because he was less of a man. Why, she had run even from Peter—good, honest, conscientious Peter, with the heart and the soul and the nerve of a man. Peter had sent her scurrying before him because of the great love he dared to have for her. Peter challenged her to take up life with him—to buck New York with him. This was after he had waded in himself with naked fists, man-fashion. That was what gave Peter his right. That right was what she feared.

Monte had a grandfather who in forty-nine crossed the plains. A picture of him hung in the Covington house in Philadelphia. The painting revealed steel-gray eyes and, even below the beard of respectability, a mouth that in many ways was like Peter's. Montague Sears Covington—that was his name; the name that had been handed down to Monte. The man had shouldered a rifle, fought his way across deserts and over mountain paths, had risked his life a dozen times a day to reach the unknown El Dorado of the West. He had done this partly for a woman—a slip of a girl in New York whom he left behind to wait for him, though she begged to go. That was Monte's grandmother.

Monte, in spite of his ancestry, had jogged along, dodging the responsibilities—the responsibilities that Peter Noyes rushed forward to meet. He had ducked even love, even fatherhood. Like any quitter on the gridiron, instead of tackling low and hard, he had side-stepped. He had seen Chic in agony, and because of that had taken the next boat for Marseilles. He had turned tail and run. He had seen Teddy, and had run to what he thought was safe cover. If he paid the cost after that, whose the fault? The least he could do now was to pay the cost like a man.

Here was the salient necessity—to pay the cost like a man. There must be no whining, no regretting, no side-stepping this time. He must make her free by surrendering all his own rights, privileges, and title. He must turn her over to Peter, who had played the game. He must do more. He must see that she went to Peter. He must accomplish something positive this time.

Beatrice had asked him to use his influence. It was slight, pitifully slight, but he must do what he could. He must plan for them, deliberately, more such opportunities as this one he had planned for them unconsciously to-day. He must give them more chances to be together. He had looked forward to having breakfast with her in the morning. He must give up that. He must keep himself in the background while he was here, and then, at the right moment, get out altogether.

Technically, he must desert her. He must make that supreme sacrifice. At the moment when he stood ready to challenge the world for her—at the moment when his heart within him burned to face for her all the dangers from which he had run—at that point he must relinquish even this privilege, and with smiling lips pose before the world and before her as a quitter. He must not even use the deserter's prerogative of running. He must leave her cheerfully and jauntily—as the care-free ass known to her and to the world as just Monte.

The scorn of those words stung him white with helpless passion. She had wished him always to be just Monte, because she thought that was the best there was in him. As such he was at least harmless—a good-natured chump to be trusted to do no harm, if he did no good. The grandson of the Covington who had faced thirst and hunger and sudden death for his woman, who had won for her a fortune fighting against other strong men, the grandson of a man who had tackled life like a man, must sacrifice his one chance to allow this ancestor to know his own as a man. He could have met him chin up with Madame Covington on his arm. He had that chance once.

How ever had he missed it? He sat there with his fists clenched between his knees, asking himself the question over and over again. He had known her for over a decade. As a school-girl he had seen her at Chic's, and now ten years later he saw that even then she had within her all that she now had. That clear, white forehead had been there then; the black arched brows, the thin, straight nose, and the mobile lips. He caught his breath as he thought of those lips. Her eyes, too—but no, a change had taken place there. He had always thought of her eyes as cold—as impenetrable. They were not that now. Once or twice he thought he had seen into them a little way. Once or twice he thought he had glimpsed gentle, fluttering figures in them. Once or twice they had been like windows in a long-closed house, suddenly flung open upon warm rooms filled with flowers. It made him dizzy now to remember those moments.

He paced his room. In another week or two, if he had kept on,—if Peter had not come,—he might have been admitted farther into that house. He squared his shoulders. If he fought for his own even now—if, man against man, he challenged Peter for her—he might have a fighting chance. Was not that his right? In New York, in the world outside New York, that was the law: a hard fight—the best man to win. In war, favors might be shown; but in life, with a man's own at stake, it was every one for himself. Peter himself would agree to that. He was not one to ask favors. A fair fight was all he demanded. Then let it be a clean, fair fight with bare knuckles to a finish. Let him show himself to Marjory as the grandson of the man who gave him his name; let him press his claims.

He was ready now to face the world with her. He was eager to do that. Neither heights nor depths held any terrors for him. He envied Chic—he envied even poor mad Hamilton.

Suddenly he saw a great truth. There is no difference between the heights and the depths to those who are playing the game. It is only those who sit in the grand-stand who see the difference. He ought to have known that. The hard throws, the stinging tackles that used to bring the grandstand to its feet, he never felt. The players knew something that those upon the seats did not know, and thrilled with a keener joy than the onlookers dreamed of.

If he could only be given another chance to do something for Marjory—something that would bite into him, something that would twist his body and maul him! If he could not face some serious physical danger for her, then some great sacrifice—

Which was precisely the opportunity now offered. He had been considering this sacrifice from his own personal point of view. He had looked upon it as merely a personal punishment. But, after all, it was for her. It was for her alone. Peter played no part in it whatever. Neither did he himself. It was for her—for her!

Monte set his jaws. If, through Peter, he could bring her happiness, then that was all the reward he could ask. Here was a man who loved her, who would be good to her and fight hard for her. He was just the sort of man he could trust her to. If he could see them settled in New York, as Chic and Mrs. Chic were settled, see them start the brave adventure, then he would have accomplished more than he had ever been able to accomplish so far.

There was no need of thinking beyond that point. What became of his life after that did not matter in the slightest. Wherever he was, he would always know that she was where she belonged, and that was enough. He must hold fast to that thought.

A knock at his door made him turn on his heels.

"Who's that?" he demanded.

"It's I—Noyes," came the answer. "Have you gone to bed yet?"

Monte swung open the door.

"Come in," he said.

"I thought I 'd like to talk with you, if it is n't too late," explained Peter nervously.

"On the contrary, you could n't have come more opportunely. I was just thinking about you."

He led Peter to a chair.

"Sit down and make yourself comfortable."

Monte lighted a cigarette, sank into a near-by chair, and waited.

"Beatrice said she told you," began Peter.

"She did," answered Monte; "I'd congratulate you if it would n't be so manifestly superfluous."

"I did n't realize she was an old friend of yours."

"I've known her for ten years," said Monte.

"It's wonderful to have known her as long as that. I envy you."

"That's strange, because I almost envy you."

Peter laughed.

"I have a notion I 'd be worried if you were n't already married, Covington."

"Worried?"

"I think Mrs. Covington must be a good deal like Marjory."

"She is," admitted Monte.

"So, if I had n't been lucky enough to find you already suited, you might have given me a race."

"You forget that the ladies themselves have some voice in such matters," Monte replied slowly.

"I have better reasons than you for not forgetting that," answered Peter.

Monte started.

"I was n't thinking of you," he put in quickly. "Besides, you did n't give Marjory a fair chance. Her aunt had just died, and she—well, she has learned a lot since then."

"She has changed!" exclaimed Peter. "I noticed it at once; but I was almost afraid to believe it. She seems steadier—more serious."

"Yes."

"You've seen a good deal of her recently?"

"For the last two or three weeks," answered Monte.

"You don't mind my talking to you about her?"

"Not at all."

"As you're an old friend of hers, I feel as if I had the right."

"Go ahead."

"It seems to me as if she had suddenly grown from a girl to a woman. I saw the woman in her all the time. It—it was to her I spoke before. Maybe, as you said, the woman was n't quite ready."

"I'm sure of it."

"You speak with conviction."

"As I told you, I've come to know her better these last few weeks than ever before. I've had a chance to study her. She's had a chance, too, to study—other men. There's been one in particular—"

Peter straightened a bit.

"One in particular?" he demanded aggressively.

"No one you need fear," replied Monte. "In a way, it's because of him that your own chances have improved."

"How?"

"It has given her an opportunity to compare him with you."

"Are you at liberty to tell me about him?"

"Yes; I think I have that right," replied Monte; "I'll not be violating any confidences, because what I know about him I know from the man himself. Furthermore, it was I who introduced him to her."

"Oh—a friend of yours."

"Not a friend, exactly; an acquaintance of long standing would be more accurate. I've been in touch with him all my life, but it's only lately I've felt that I was really getting to know him."

"Is he here in Nice now?" inquired Peter.

"No," answered Monte slowly. "He went away a little while ago. He went suddenly—God knows where. I don't think he will ever come back."

"You can't help pitying the poor devil if he was fond of her," said Peter.

"But he was n't good enough for her. It was his own fault too, so he is n't deserving even of pity."

"Probably that makes it all the harder. What was the matter with him?"

"He was one of the kind we spoke of the other night—the kind who always sits in the grandstand instead of getting into the game."

"Pardon me if I'm wrong, but—I thought you spoke rather sympathetically of that kind the other night."

"I was probably reflecting his views," Monte parried.

"That accounts for it," returned Peter. "Somehow, it did n't sound consistent in you. I wish I could see your face, Covington."

- 130 -

"We're sitting in the dark here," answered Monte.

"Go on."

"Marjory liked this fellow well enough because—well, because he looked more or less like a man. He was big physically, and all that. Besides, his ancestors were all men, and I suppose they handed down something."

"What was his name?"

"I think I'd rather not tell you that. It's of no importance. This is all strictly in confidence."

"I understand."

"So she let herself see a good deal of him. He was able to amuse her. That kind of fellow generally can entertain a woman. In fact, that is about all they are good for. When it comes down to the big things, there is n't much there. They are well enough for the holidays, and I guess that was all she was thinking about. She had had a hard time, and wanted amusement. Maybe she fancied that was all she ever wanted; but—well, there was more in her than she knew herself."

"A thousand times more!" exclaimed Peter.

"She found it out. Perhaps, after all, this fellow served his purpose in helping her to realize that."

"Perhaps."

"So, after that, he left."

"And he cared for her?"

"Yes."

"Poor devil!"

"I don't know," mused Monte. "He seemed, on the whole, rather glad that he had been able to do that much for her."

"I'd like to meet that man some day. I have a notion there is more in him than you give him credit for, Covington."

"I doubt it."

"A man who would give up her—"

"She's the sort of woman a man would want to do his level best for," broke in Monte. "If that meant giving her up,—if the fellow felt he was n't big enough for her,—then he could n't do anything else, could he?"

"The kind big enough to consider that would be big enough for her," declared Peter.

Monte drew a quick breath.

"Do you mind repeating that?"

"I say the man really loving her who would make such a sacrifice comes pretty close to measuring up to her standard."

"I think he would like to hear that. You see, it's the first real sacrifice he ever undertook."

"It may be the making of him."

"Perhaps."

"He'll always have her before him as an ideal. When you come in touch with such a woman as she—you can't lose, Covington, no matter how things turn out."

"I 'll tell him that too."

"It's what I tell myself over and over again. To-day—well, I had an idea there must be some one in the background of her life I did n't know about."

"You 'd better get that out of your head. This man is n't even in the background, Noyes."

"I 'm not so sure. I thought she seemed worried. I tried to make her tell me, but she only laughed. She'd face death with a smile, that woman. I got to thinking about it in my room, and that's why I came down here to you. You've seen more of her these last few months than I have."

"Not months; only weeks."

"And this other—I don't want to pry into her affairs, but we're all just looking to her happiness, are n't we?"

"Consider this other man as dead and gone," cut in Monte. "He was lucky to be able to play the small part in her life that he did play."

"But something is disturbing her. I know her voice; I know her laugh. If I did n't have those to go by, there'd be something else. I can *feel* when she's herself and when she is n't."

Monte grasped his chair arms. He had studied her closely the last few days, and had not been able to detect the fact that she was worried. He had thought her gayer, more light-hearted, than usual. It was so that she had held herself before him. If Peter was right,—and Monte did not doubt the man's superior intuition,—then obviously she was worrying over the technicality that still held her a prisoner. Until she was actually free she would live up to the letter of her contract. This would naturally tend to strain her intercourse with Peter. She was not one to take such things lightly.

Monte rose, crossed the room, and placed his hand on Peter's shoulder.

"I think I can assure you," he said slowly, "that if there is anything bothering her now, it is nothing that will last. All you've got to do is to be patient and hold on."

"You seem to be mighty confident."

"If you knew what I know, you'd be confident too."

Peter frowned.

"I don't like discussing these things, but—they mean so much."

"So much to all of us," nodded Monte. "Now, the thing to do is to turn in and get a good night's sleep. After all, there *is* something in keeping normal."

CHAPTER XXI
BACK TO SCHEDULE

Monte rose the next morning to find the skies leaden and a light, drizzling rain falling that promised to continue all day. It was the sort of weather that ordinarily left him quite helpless, because, not caring for either bridge or billiards, nothing remained but to pace the hotel piazza—an amusement that under the most favorable conditions has its limitations. But to-day—even though the rain had further interfered with his arrangements by making it necessary to cancel the trip he had planned for Marjory and Peter to Cannes—the weather was an inconsequential incident. It did not matter greatly to him whether it rained or not.

Not that he was depressed to indifference. Rather he was conscious of a certain nervous excitement akin to exhilaration that he had not felt since the days of the big games, when he used to get up with his blood tingling in heady anticipation of the task before him. He took his plunge with hearty relish, and rubbed his body until it glowed with the Turkish towel.

His arm was free of the sling now, and, though it was still a bit stiff, it was beginning to limber up nicely. In another week it would be as good as new, with only a slight scar left to serve as a reminder of the episode that had led to so much. In time that too would disappear; and then— But he was not concerned with the future. That, any more than the weather, was no affair of his.

This morning Marjory would perforce remain indoors, and so if he went to see her it was doubtful whether he would be interfering with any plans she might have made for Peter. An hour was all he needed—perhaps less. This would leave the two the remainder of the day free—and, after that, all the days to come. There would be hundreds of them—all the days of the summer, all the days of the fall, all the days of the winter, and all the days of the spring; then another summer, and so a new cycle full of days twenty-four hours long.

Out of these he was going to take one niggardly hour. Nor was he asking that little for his own sake. Eager as he was—as he had been for two weeks—for the privilege of just being alone with her, he would have foregone that now, had it been possible to write her what he had to say. In a letter it is easy to leave unsaid so many things. But he must face her leaving the same things unsaid, because she was a woman who demanded that a man speak what he had to say man-fashion. He must do that, even though there would be little truth in his words. He must make her believe the lie. He cringed at the word. But, after all, it was the truth to her. That was what he must keep always in mind. He had only to help her keep her own conception. He was coming to her, not in his proper person, but as just Monte. As such he would be telling the truth.

He shaved and dressed with some care. The rain beat against the window, and he did not hear it. He went down to breakfast and faced the vacant chair which he had ordered to be left at his table. She had never sat there, though at every meal it stood ready for her. Peter suggested once that he join them at their table until madame returned; but Monte had shaken his head.

Monte did not telephone her until ten, and then he asked simply if he might come over for an hour.

"Certainly," she answered: "I shall be glad to see you. It's a miserable day, Monte."

"It's raining a bit, but I don't mind."

"That's because you're so good-natured."

He frowned. It was a privilege he had over the telephone.

"Anyhow, what you can't help you may as well grin and bear."

"I suppose so, Monte," she answered. "But if I 'm to grin, I must depend upon you to make me."

"I'll be over in five minutes," he replied.

She needed him to make her grin! That was all he was good for. Thank Heaven, he had it in his power to do this much; as soon as he told her she was to be free again, the smile would return to her lips.

He went at once to the hotel, and she came down to meet him, looking very serious—and very beautiful. Her deep eyes seemed deeper than ever, perhaps because of a trace of dark below them. She had color, but it was bright crimson against a dead white. Her lips were more mobile than usual, as if she were having difficulty in controlling them—as if many unspoken things were struggling there for expression.

When he took her warm hand, she raised her head a little, half closing her eyes. It was clear that she was worrying more than even he had suspected. Poor little woman, her conscience was probably harrying the life out of her. This must not be.

They went upstairs to the damp, desolate sun parlor, and he undertook at once the business in hand.

"It has n't worked very well, has it, Marjory?" he began, with a forced smile.

Turning aside her head, she answered in a voice scarcely above a whisper:—

"No, Monte."

"But," he went on, "there's no sense in getting stirred up about that."

"It was such a—a hideous mistake," she said.

"That's where you're wrong," he declared. "We've tried a little experiment, and it failed. Is n't that all there is to it?"

"All?"

"Absolutely all," he replied. "What we did n't reckon with was running across old friends who would take the adventure so seriously. If we'd only gone to Central Africa or Asia Minor—"

"It would have been just the same if we'd gone to the North Pole," she broke in.

"You think so?"

"I know it. Women can't trifle with—with such things without getting hurt."

"I 'm sorry. I suppose I should have known."

"You were just trying to be kind, Monte," she answered. "Don't take any of the blame. It's all mine."

"I urged you."

"What of that?" she demanded. "It was for me to come or not to come. That is one part of her life over which a woman has absolute control. I came because I was so utterly selfish I did not realize what I was doing."

"And I?" he asked quickly.

"You?"

She turned and tried to meet his honest eyes.

"I'm afraid I've spoiled your holiday," she murmured.

He clinched his jaws against the words that surged to his lips.

"If we could leave those last few weeks just as they were—" he said. "Can't we call that evening I met you in Paris the beginning, and the day we reached Nice the end?"

"Only there is no end," she cried.

"Let the day we reached the Hôtel des Roses be the end. I should like to go away feeling that the whole incident up to then was something detached from the rest of our lives."

"You're going—where?" she gasped.

He tried to smile.

"I 'll have to pick up my schedule again."

"You're going—when?"

"In a day or two now," he replied. "You see—it's necessary for me to desert you."

"Monte!"

"The law demands the matter of six months' absence—perhaps a little longer. I 'll have this looked up and will notify you. Desertion is an ugly word; but, after all, it sounds better than cruel and abusive treatment."

"It's I who deserted," she said.

He waved the argument aside.

"Anyway, it's only a technicality. The point is that I must show the world that—that we did not mean what we said. So I 'll go on to England."

"And play golf," she added for him.

He nodded.

"I 'll probably put up a punk game. Never was much good at golf. But it will help get me back into the rut. Then I 'll sail about the first of August for New York and put a few weeks into camp."

"Then you'll go on to Cambridge."

"And hang around until after the Yale game."

"Then—"

"How many months have I been gone already?"

"Four."

"Oh, yes; then I'll go back to New York."

"What will you do there, Monte?"

"I—I don't know. Maybe I'll call on Chic some day."

"If they should ever learn!" cried Marjory.

"Eh?"

Monte passed his hand over his forehead.

"There is n't any danger of that, is there?"

"I don't think I'll ever dare meet *her* again."

Monte squared his shoulders.

"See here, little woman; you must n't feel this way. It won't do at all. That's why I thought if you could only separate these last few weeks from everything else—just put them one side and go from there—it would be so much better. You see, we've got to go on and—holy smoke! this has got to be as if it never happened. You have your life ahead of you and I have mine. We can't let this spoil all the years ahead. You—why, you—"

She looked up. It was a wonder he did not take her in his arms in that moment. He held himself as he had once held himself when eleven men were trying to push him and his fellows over the last three yards separating them from a goal.

"It's necessary to go on, is n't it?" he repeated helplessly.

"Yes, yes," she answered quickly. "You must go back to your schedule just as soon as ever you can. As soon as we're over the ugly part—"

"The divorce?"

"As soon as we're over that, everything will be all right again," she nodded.

"Surely," he agreed.

"But we must n't remember anything. That's quite impossible. The thing to do is to forget."

She appeared so earnest that he hastened to reassure her.

"Then we'll forget."

He said it so cheerfully, she was ready to believe him.

"That ought to be easy for you," he added.

"For me?"

"I 'm going to leave you with Peter."

She caught her breath. She did not dare answer.

"I've seen a good deal of him lately," he continued. "We've come to know each other rather intimately, as sometimes men do in a short while when they have interests in common."

"You and Peter have interests in common!" she exclaimed.

He appeared uneasy.

"We're both Harvard, you know."

"I see."

"Of course, I've had to do more or less hedging on account—of Madame Covington."

"I'm sorry, Monte."

"You need n't be, because it was she who introduced me to him. And, I tell you, he's fine and big and worth while all through. But you know that."

"Yes."

"That's why I'm going to feel quite safe about leaving you with him."

She started. That word "safe" was like a stab with a penknife. She would have rather had him strike her a full blow in the face than use it. Yet, in its miserable fashion, it expressed all that he had sought through her—all that she had allowed him to seek. From the first they had each sought safety, because they did not dare face the big things.

Now, at the moment she was ready, the same weakness that she had encouraged in him was helping take him away from her. And the pitiful tragedy of it was that Peter was helping too, and then challenging her to accept still graver dangers through him. It was a pitiful tangle, and yet one that she must allow to continue.

"You mean he'll help you not to worry about me?"

"That's it," he nodded. "Because I've seen the man side of him, and it's even finer than the side you see."

Her lips came together.

"There's no reason why you should feel responsibility for me even without Peter," she protested.

She was seated in one of the wicker chairs, chin in hand. He stepped toward her.

"You don't think I'd be cad enough to desert my wife actually?" he demanded.

He seemed so much in earnest that for a second the color flushed the chalk-white portions of her cheeks.

"Sit down, Monte," she pleaded. "I—I did n't expect you to take it like that. I'm afraid Peter is making you too serious. After all, you know, I'm of age. I'm not a child."

He sat down, bending toward her.

"We've both acted more or less like children," he said gently. "Now I guess the time has come for us to grow up. Peter will help you do that."

"And you?"

"He has helped me already. And when he gets his eyes back—"

"You think there is a chance for that?"

"Just one chance," he answered.

"Oh!" she cried.

"It's a big opportunity," he said.

She rose and went to the window, where she looked out upon the gray ocean and the slanting rain and a world grown dull and sodden. He followed her there, but with his shoulders erect now.

"I'm going now," he said. "I think I shall take the night train for Paris. I want to leave the machine—the machine we came down here in—for you."

"Don't—please don't."

"It's for you and Peter. The thing for you both to do is to get out in it every day."

"I—I don't want to."

"You mean—"

He placed his hand upon her arm, and she ventured one more look into his eyes. He was frowning. She must not allow that. She must send him away in good spirits. That was the least she could do. So she forced a smile.

"All right," she promised; "if it will make you more comfortable."

"It would worry me a lot if I thought you were n't going to be happy."

"I'll go out every fair day."

"That's fine."

He took a card from his pocket and scribbled his banker's address upon it.

"If anything should come up where—where I can be of any use, you can always reach me through this address."

She took the card. Even to the end he was good—good and four-square. He was so good that her throat ached. She could not endure this very much longer. He extended his hand.

"S'long and good luck," he said.

"I—I hope your golf will be better than you think."

Then he said a peculiar thing. He seldom swore, and seldom lost his head as completely as he did that second. But, looking her full in the eyes, he ejaculated below his breath:—

"Damn golf!"

The observation was utterly irrelevant. Turning, he clicked his heels together like a soldier and went out. The door closed behind him. For a second her face was illumined as with a great joy. In a sort of ecstasy, she repeated his words.

"He said," she whispered—"he said, 'Damn golf.'" Then she threw herself into a wicker chair and began to sob.

"Oh!" she choked. "If—if—"

CHAPTER XXII
A CONFESSION

Monte left Nice on the twentieth of July, to join—as Peter supposed—Madame Covington in Paris. Monte himself had been extremely ambiguous about his destination, being sure of only one fact: that he should not return inside of a year, if he did then. Peter had asked for his address, and Monte had given him the same address that he gave Marjory.

"I want to keep in touch with you," Peter said.

Peter missed the man. On the ride with Marjory that he enjoyed the next day after Monte's departure, he talked a great deal of him.

"I 'd like to have seen into his eyes," he told her. "I kept feeling I 'd find something there more than I got hold of in his voice and the grip of his hand."

"He has blue eyes," she told him, "and they are clean as a child's."

"They are a bit sad?"

"Monte's eyes sad?" she exclaimed. "What made you think so?"

"Perhaps because, from what he let drop the other night, I gathered he was n't altogether happy with Mrs. Covington."

"He told you that?"

"No; not directly," he assured her. "He's too loyal. I may be utterly mistaken; only he was rather vague as to why she was not here with him."

"She was not with him," Marjory answered slowly. "She was not with him because she was n't big enough to deserve him."

"Then it's a fact there's a tragedy in his life?"

"Not in his—in hers," she answered passionately.

"How can that be?"

"Because she's the one who realizes the truth."

"But she's the one who went away."

"Because of that. It's a miserable story, Peter."

"You knew her intimately?"

"A great many years."

"I think Covington said he had known you a long time."

"Yes."

"Then, knowing her and knowing him, was n't there anything you could do?"

"I did what I could," she answered wearily.

"Perhaps that explains why he hurried back to her."

"He has n't gone to her. He'll never go back to her. She deserted him, and now—he's going to make it permanent."

"A divorce?"

"Yes, Peter," she answered, with a little shiver.

"You're taking it hard."

"I know all that he means to her," she choked.

"She loves him?"

"With all her heart and soul."

"And he does n't know it?"

"Why, he would n't believe it—if she told him. She can never let him know it. She'd deny it if he asked her. She loves him enough for that."

"Good Lord!" exclaimed Peter. "There's a mistake there somewhere."

"The mistake came first," she ran on. "Oh, I don't know why I'm telling you these things, except that it is a relief to tell them to some one."

"Tell me all about it," he encouraged her. "I knew there was something on your mind."

"Peter," she said earnestly, "can you imagine a woman so selfish that she wanted to marry just to escape the responsibilities of marriage?"

"It is n't possible," he declared.

Her cheeks were a vivid scarlet. Had he been able to see them, she could not have gone on.

"A woman so selfish," she faltered ahead, "that she preferred a make-believe husband to a real husband, because—because so she thought she would be left free."

"Free for what?" he demanded.

"To live."

"When love and marriage and children are all there is to life?" he asked.

She caught her breath.

"You see, she did not know that then. She thought all those things called for the sacrifice of her freedom."

"What freedom?" he demanded again. "It's when we're alone that we're slaves—slaves to ourselves. A woman alone, a man alone, living to himself alone—what is there for him? He can only go around and around in a pitifully small circle—a circle that grows smaller and smaller with every year. Between twenty and thirty a man can exhaust all there is in life for himself alone. He has eaten and slept and traveled and played until his senses have become dull. Perhaps a woman lasts a little longer, but not much longer. Then they are locked away in themselves until they die."

"Peter!" she cried in terror.

"It's only as we live in others that we live forever," he ran on. "It is only by toiling and sacrificing and suffering and loving that we become immortal. It is so we acquire real freedom."

"Yes, Peter," she agreed, with a gasp.

"Could n't you make her understand that?"

"She does understand. That's the pity of it."

"And Covington?"

"It's in him to understand; only—she lost the right to make him understand. She—she debased herself. So she must sacrifice herself to get clean again. She must make even greater sacrifices than any she cowed away from. She must do this without any of the compensations that come to those who have been honest and unafraid."

"What of him?"

"He must never know. He'll go round and round his little circle, and she must watch him."

"It's terrible," he murmured. "It will be terrible for her to watch him do that. If you had told him how she felt—"

"God forbid!"

"Or if you had only told me, so that I could have told him—"

She seized Peter's arm.

"You would n't have dared!"

"I'd dare anything to save two people from such torment."

"You—you don't think he will worry?"

"I think he is worrying a great deal."

"Only for the moment," she broke in. "But soon—in a week or two—he will be quite himself again. He has a great many things to do. He has tennis and—and golf."

She checked herself abruptly. ("Damn golf!" Monte had said.)

"There's too much of a man in him now to be satisfied with such things," said Peter. "It's a pity—it's a pity there are not two of you, Marjory."

"Of me?"

"He thinks a great deal of you. If he had met you before he met this other—"

"What are you saying, Peter?"

"That you're the sort of woman who could have called out in him an honest love."

There, beside Peter who could not see, Marjory bent low and buried her face in her hands.

"You 're the sort of woman," he went on, "who could have roused the man in him that has been waiting all this time for some one like you."

How Peter was hurting her! How he was pinching her with red-hot irons! It hurt so much that she was glad. Here, at last, she was beginning her sacrifice for Monte. So she made neither moan nor groan, nor covered her ears, but took her punishment like a man.

"Some one else must do all that," she said.

"Yes," he answered. "Or his life will be wasted. He needs to suffer. He needs to give up. This thing we call a tragedy may be the making of him."

"For some one else," she repeated.

Peter was fumbling about for her hand. Suddenly she straightened herself.

"It must be for some one else," he said hoarsely—"because I want you for myself. In time—you must be mine. With the experience of those two before us, we must n't make the same mistake ourselves. I—I was n't going to tell you this until I had my eyes back. But, heart o' mine, I 've held in so long. Here in the dark one gets so much alone. And being alone is what kills."

She was hiding her hand from him.

"I can't find your hand," he whispered, like a child lost in the dark.

Summoning all her strength, she placed her hand within his. "It is cold!" he cried.

Yet the day was warm. They were speeding through a sunlighted country of olive trees and flowers in bloom—a warm world and tender.

He drew her fingers to his lips and kissed them passionately. She suffered it, closing her eyes against the pain.

"I've wanted you so all these months!" he cried. "I should n't have let you go in the first place. I should n't have let you go."

"No, Peter," she answered.

"And now that I've found you again, you'll stay?"

He was lifting his face to hers—straining to see her. To have answered any way but as he pleaded would have been to strike that upturned face.

"I—I 'll try to stay," she faltered.

"I 'll make you!" he breathed. "I 'll hold you tight, soul of mine. Would you—would you kiss my eyes?"

Holding her breath, Marjory lightly brushed each of his eyes with her lips.

"It's like balm," he whispered. "I've dreamed at night of this."

"Every day I'll do it," she said. "Only—for a little while—you 'll not ask for anything more, Peter?"

"Not until some day they open—in answer to that call," he replied.

"I did n't mean that, Peter," she said hurriedly. "Only I'm so mixed up myself."

"It's so new to you," he nodded. "To me it's like a day foreseen a dozen years. Long before I saw you I knew I was getting ready for you. Now—what do a few weeks matter?"

"It may be months, Peter, before I'm quite steady."

"Even if it's years," he exclaimed, "I've felt your lips."

"Only on your eyes," she cried in terror.

"I—I would n't dare to feel them except on my eyes—for a little while. Even there they take away my breath."

CHAPTER XXIII
LETTERS

Letter from Peter Noyes to Monte Covington, received by the latter at the Hôtel Normandie, Paris, France:—

NICE, FRANCE, July 22.

Dear Covington:—

I don't know whether you can make out this scrawl, because I have to feel my way across the paper; but I'm sitting alone in my room, aching to talk with you as we used to talk. If you were here I know you would be glad to listen, because—suddenly all I told you about has come true.

Riding to Cannes the very next day after you left, I spoke to her and—she listened. It was all rather vague and she made no promises, but she listened. In a few weeks or months or years, now, she'll be mine for all time. She does n't want me to tell Beatrice, and there is no one else to tell except you—so forgive me, old man, if I let myself loose.

Besides, in a way, you're responsible. We were talking of you, because we missed you. You have a mighty good friend in her, Covington. She knows you—the real you that I thought only I had glimpsed. She sees the man in the game—not the man in the grand-stand. Her Covington is the man they used to give nine long Harvards for. I never heard that in front of my name. I was a grind—a "greasy grind," they used to call me. It did n't hurt, for I smiled in rather a superior sort of way at the men I thought were wasting their energy on the gridiron. But, after all, you fellows got something out of it that the rest of us did n't get. A 'Varsity man remains a 'Varsity man all his life. To-day you stand before her as a 'Varsity man. I think she always thinks of you as in a red sweater with a black "H." Any time that you feel you're up against anything hard, that ought to help you.

We talked a great deal of you, as I said, and I find myself now thinking more of you than of myself in connection with her. I don't understand it. Perhaps it's because she seems so alone in the world, and you are the most intimate friend she has. Perhaps it's because you've seen so much more of her than I in these last few months. Anyway, I have a feeling that somehow you are an integral part of her. I've tried to puzzle out the relationship, and I can't. "Brother" does not define it; neither does "comrade." If you were not already married, I'd almost suspect her of being in love with you.

I know that sounds absurd. I know it is absurd. She is n't the kind to allow her emotions to get away from her like that. But I'll say this much, Covington: that if we three were to start fresh, I'd stand a mighty poor chance with her.

This is strange talk from a man who less than six hours ago became officially engaged. I told her that I had let her go once, and that now I had found her again I wanted her to stay. And she said, "I'll try." That was n't very much, Covington, was it? But I seized the implied promise as a drowning man does a straw. It was so much more than anything I have hoped for.

I should have kept her that time I found her on the little farm in Connecticut. If I had been a little more insistent then, I think she would have come with me. But I was afraid of her money. It was rumored that her aunt left her a vast fortune, and—you know the mongrels that hound a girl in that position, Covington? I was afraid she might think I was one of the pack. She was frightened—bewildered. I should have snatched her away from them all and gone off with her. I was earning enough to support her decently, and I should have thought of nothing else. Instead of that I held back a little, and so lost her, as I thought. She sailed away, and I returned to my work like a madman—and I nearly died.

Now I feel alive clear to my finger-tips. I 'm going to get my eyes back. I have n't the slightest doubt in the world about that. Already I feel the magic of the new balm that has been applied. They don't ache any more. Sitting here to-night without my shade, I can hold them open and catch the feeble light that filters in from the street lamps at a distance. It is only a question of a few months, perhaps weeks, perhaps days. The next time we meet I shall be able to see you.

You won't object to hearing a man rave a little, Covington? If you do, you can tear up this right here. But I know I can't say anything good about Marjory that you won't agree with. Maybe, however, you'd call my present condition abnormal. Perhaps it is; but I wonder if it is n't part of every normal man's life to be abnormal to this extent at least once—to see, for once, this staid old world through the eyes of a prince of the ancient city of Bagdad; to thrill with the magic and gorgeous beauty of it? It shows what might always be, if one were poet enough to sustain the mood.

Here am I, a plugging lawyer of the Borough of Manhattan, City of New York, State of New York—which is just about as far away from the city of Bagdad as you can get. I'm concerned mainly with certain details of corporation law—the structure of soulless business institutions which were never heard of in Bagdad. My daily path takes me from certain uptown bachelor quarters through the subway to a certain niche in a downtown cave dwelling. Then—presto, she comes. I pass over all that intervened, because it is no longer important, but—presto again, I find myself here a prince in some royal castle of Bagdad, counting the moments until another day breaks and I can feel the touch of my princess's hand. Even my dull eyes count for me, because so I can fancy myself, if I choose, in some royal apartment, surrounded by hanging curtains of silk, priceless marbles, and ornaments of gold and silver, with many silent eunuchs awaiting my commands. From my windows I'm at liberty to imagine towers and minarets and domes of copper.

Always she, my princess, is somewhere in the background, when she is not actually by my side. When I saw her before, Covington, I marveled at her eyes—those deep, wonderful eyes that told you so little and made you dream so much. I saw her hair too, and her straight nose, and her beautiful lips. Those things I see now as I saw them then. I must wait a little while really to see them again. In their place, however, I have now her voice and the sound of her footsteps. To hear her coming, just to hear the light fall of her feet upon the ground, is like music.

But when she speaks, Covington, then all other sounds cease, and she speaks alone to me in a world grown silent to listen. There is some quality in that voice that gets into me—that reaches and vibrates certain hidden strings I did not know were there. So sweet is the music that I can hardly give enough attention to make out the meaning of her words. What she says does not so much matter as that she should be speaking to me—to my ears alone.

And these things are merely the superficialities of her. There still remains the princess herself below these wonderful externals. There still remains the woman herself. Woman, any woman, is marvelous enough, Covington. When you think of all they stand for, the fineness of them compared with our man grossness, that wonderful power of creation in them, their exquisite delicacy, combined with the big-souled capacity for sacrifice and suffering that dwarfs any of our petty burdens into insignificance—God knows, a man should bow his knee before the least of them. But when to all those general attributes of the sex you add that something more born in a woman like Marjory—what in the world can a man do big enough to deserve the charge of such a soul? In the midst of all my princely emotions, that thought makes me humble, Covington.

I fear I have rambled a good deal, old man. I can't read over what I have been scribbling here, so I must let it go as it is. But I wanted to tell you some of these things that are rushing through my head all the time, because I knew you would be glad for me and glad for her. Or does my own joy result in such supreme selfishness that I am tempted to intrude it upon others? I don't believe so, because there is no one else in the world to whom I would venture to write as I 've written to you.

I'm not asking you to answer, because what I should want to hear from you I would n't allow any one else to read. So tear this up and forget it if you want. Some day I shall meet you again and see you. Then I can talk to you face to face.

Yours,
PETER J. NOYES.

Sitting alone in his room at the Normandie, Monte read this through. Then his hands dropped to his side and the letter fell from them to the floor.

"Oh, my God!" he said. "Oh, my God!"

Letter from Madame Covington to her husband, Monte Covington, which the latter never received at all because it was never sent. It was never meant to be sent. It was written merely to save herself from doing something rash, something for which she could never forgive herself—like taking the next train to Paris and claiming this man as if he were her own:—

Dearest Prince of my Heart:—

You've been gone from me twelve hours. For twelve hours you've left me here all alone. I don't know how I've lived. I don't know how I'm going to get through the night and to-morrow. Only there won't be any to-morrow. There'll never be anything more than periods of twelve hours, until you come back: just from dawn to dark, and then from dark to dawn, over and over again. Each period must be fought through as it comes, with no thought about the others. I'm beginning on the third. The morning will bring the fourth.

Each one is like a lifetime—a birth and a death. And oh, my Prince, I shall soon be very, very old. I don't dare look in the mirror to-night, for fear of seeing how old I've grown since morning. I remember a word they used on shipboard when the waves threw the big propeller out of the water and the full power of the engines was wasted on air. They called it "racing." It was bad for the ship to have this energy go for nothing. It racked her and made her tremble and groan. I've been racing ever since you went, churning the air to no purpose, with a power that was meant to drive me ahead. I'm right where I started after it all.

Dearest heart of mine, I love you. Though I tremble away from those words, I must put them down for once in black and white. Though I tear them up into little pieces so small that no one can read them, I must write them once. It is such a relief, here by myself, to be honest. If you were here and I were honest, I'd stand very straight and look you fair in the eyes and tell you that over and over again. "I love you, Monte," I would say. "I love you with all my heart and soul, Monte," I would say. "Right or wrong, coward that I am or not, whether it is good for you or not, I love you, Monte," I would say. And, if you wished, I would let you kiss me. And, if you would let me, I would kiss you on your dear tousled hair, on your forehead, on your eyes—

That is where I kissed Peter to-day. I will tell you here, as I would tell you standing before you. I kissed Peter on his eyes, and I have promised to kiss him again upon his eyes to-morrow—if to-morrow comes. I did it because he said it would help him to see again. And if he sees again—why, Monte, if he sees again, then he will see how absurd it is that he should ask me to love him.

Blind as he is, he almost saw that to-day, when he made me promise to try to stay by his side. With his eyes full open, then he will be able to read my eyes. So I shall kiss him there as often as he wishes. Then, when he understands, I shall not fear for him. He is a man. Only, if I told him with my lips, he would not understand. He must find out for himself. Then he will throw back his shoulders and take the blow—as we all of us have had to take our blows. It will be no worse for him than for you, dear, or for me.

It is not as I kissed him that I should kiss you. How silly it is of men to ask for kisses when, if they come at all, they come unasked. What shall I do with all of mine that are for you alone? I throw them out across the dark to you— here and here and here.

I wonder what you are doing at this moment? I have wondered so about every moment since you went. Because I cannot know, I feel as if I were being robbed. At times I fancy I can see as clearly as if I were with you. You went to the station and bought your ticket and got into your compartment. I could see you sitting there smoking, your eyes turned out the window. I could see what you saw, but I could not tell of what you were thinking. And that is what counts. That is the only thing that counts. There are those about me who watch me going my usual way, but how little they know of what a change has come over me! How little even Peter knows, who imagines he knows me so well.

I see you reaching Paris and driving to your hotel. I wonder if you are at the Normandie. I don't even know that. I'd like to know that. I wonder if you would dare sleep in your old room. Oh, I'd like to know that. It would be so restful to think of you there. But what, if there, are you thinking about? About me, at all? I don't want you to think about me, but I 'd die if I knew you did *not* think about me.

I don't want you to be worried, dear you. I won't have you unhappy. You said once, "Is n't it possible to care a little without caring too much?" Now I 'm going to ask you: "Is n't it possible for you to think of me a little without thinking too much?" If you could remember some of those evenings on the ride to Nice,—even if with a smile,—that would be better than nothing. If you could remember that last night before we got to Nice, when—when I looked up at you and something almost leaped from my eyes to yours. If you could remember that with just a little knowledge of what it meant—not enough to make you unhappy, but enough to make you want to see me again. Could you do that without getting uncomfortable—without mixing up your schedule?

I cried a little right here, Monte. It was a silly thing to do. But you're alone in Paris, where we were together, and I'm alone here. It is still raining. I think it is going to rain forever. I can't imagine ever seeing the blue sky again. If I did, it would only make me think of those glorious days between Paris and Nice. How wonderful it was that it never rained at all. The sky was always pink in the east when I woke up, and we saw it grow pink again at night, side by side. Then the purple of the night, with the myriad silver stars, each one beautiful in itself.

At night you always seemed to me to grow bigger than ever—inches taller and broader, until some evenings when I bade you good-night I was almost afraid of you. Because as you grew bigger I grew smaller. I used to think that, if you took a notion to do so, you'd just pick me up and carry me off. If you only had!

If you had only said, "We'll quit this child's play. You'll come with me and we'll make a home and settle down, like Chic."

I'd have been a good wife to you, Monte. Honest, I would—if you'd done like that any time before I met Peter and became ashamed. Up to that point I'd have gone with you if you had loved me enough to take me. Only, you did n't love me. That was the trouble, Monte. I'd made you think I did not want to be loved. Then I made you think I was n't worth loving. Then, when Peter came and made me see and hang my head,—why, then it was too late, even though you had wanted to take me.

But you don't know, and never will know, what a good wife I'd have been. But I would have tried to lead you a little, too. I would have watched over you and been at your command, but I would have tried to guide you into doing something worth while.

Perhaps we could have done something together worth while. You have a great deal of money, Monte, and I have a great deal. We have more than is good for us. I think if we had worked together we could have done something for other people with it. I never thought of that until lately; but the other evening, after you had been talking about your days in college, I lay awake in bed, thinking how nice it would be if we could do something for some of the young fellows there now who do not have money enough. I imagined myself going back to Cambridge with you some day and calling on the president or the dean, and hearing you say to him: "Madame Covington and I have decided that we want to help every year one or more young men needing help. If you will send to us those you approve of, we will lend them enough to finish their course."

I thought it would be nicer to lend the money than give it to them, because they would feel better about it. And they could be as long as they wished in paying it back, or if they fell into hard luck need never pay it back.

So every year we would start as many as we could, each of us paying half. They would come to us, and we would get to know them, and we would watch them through, and after that watch them fight the good fight. Why, in no time, Monte, we would have quite a family to watch over; and they would come to you for advice, and perhaps sometimes to me. Think what an interest that would add to your life! It would be so good for you, Monte. And good for me, too. Even if we had—oh, Monte, we might in time have had boys of our own in Harvard too! Then they would have selected other boys for us, and that would have been good for them too.

Here by myself I can tell you these things, because—because, God keep me, you cannot hear. You did not think I could dream such dreams as those, did you? You thought I was always thinking of myself and my own happiness, and of nothing else. You thought I asked everything and wished to give nothing. But that was before I knew what love is. That was before you touched me with the magic wand. That was before I learned that our individual lives are as brief as the sparks that fly upward, except as we live them through others; and that then—they are eternal. It was within our grasp, Monte, dear, and we trifled with it and let it go.

No, not you. It was I who refused the gift. Some day it will come to you again, through some other. That is what I tell myself over and over again. I don't think men are like women. They do not give so much of themselves, and so they may choose from two or three. So in time, as you wander about, you will find some one who will hold out her arms, and you will come. She will give you everything she has,—all honest women do that,—but it will not be all I would have given. You may think so, and so be happy; but it will not be true. I shall always know the difference. And you will give her what you have, but it will not be what you would have given me—what I would have drawn out of you. I shall always know that. Because, as I love you, heart of me, I would have found in you treasures that were meant for me alone.

I'm getting wild. I must stop. My head is spinning. Soon it will be dawn, and I am to ride again with Peter to-morrow. I told you I would ride every fair day with him, and I am hoping it will rain. But it will not rain, though to me the sky may be murky. I can see the clouds scudding before a west wind. It will be clear, and I shall ride with him as I promised, and I shall kiss him upon his eyes. But if you were with me—

Here and here and here I throw them out into the dark.

Good-night, soul of my soul.

CHAPTER XXIV
THE BLIND SEE

Day by day Peter's eyes grew stronger, because day by day he was thinking less about himself and more about Marjory.

"He needs to get away from himself," the doctors had told Beatrice. "If you can find something that will occupy his thoughts, so that he will quit thinking about his eyes, you 'll double his chances." Beatrice had done that when she found Marjory, and now she was more than satisfied with the result and with herself. Every morning she saw Peter safely entrusted to Marjory's care, and this left her free the rest of the day to walk a little, read her favorite books, and nibble chocolates. She was getting a much-needed rest, secure in the belief that everything was working out in quite an ideal way.

The only thing that seemed to her at all strange was a sudden reluctance on Peter's part to talk to her of Marjory. At the end of the day the three had dinner together at the Hôtel d'Angleterre,—Marjory could never be persuaded to dine at the Roses,—and when by eight Peter and his sister returned to their own hotel, he gave her only the barest details of his excursion, and retired early to his room. But he seemed cheerful enough, so that, after all, this might be only another favorable symptom of his progress. Peter always had been more or less secretive, and until his illness neither she nor his parents knew more than an outline of his life in New York. Periodically they came on to visit him for a few days, and periodically he went home for a few days. He was making a name for himself, and they were very proud of him, and the details did not matter. Knowing Peter as they did, it was easy enough to fill them in.

Even with Marjory, Peter talked less and less about himself. From his own ambitions, hopes, and dreams he turned more and more to hers. Now that he had succeeded in making her a prisoner, however slender the thread by which he held her, he seemed intent upon filling in all the past as fully as possible. Up to a certain point that was easy enough. She was willing to talk of her girlhood; of her father, whom she adored; and even of Aunt Kitty, who had claimed her young womanhood. She was even eager. It afforded her a safe topic in which she found relief. It gave her an opportunity also to justify, in a fashion, or at least to explain, both to herself and Peter, the frame of mind that led her up to later events.

"I ran away from you, Peter," she admitted.

"I know," he answered.

"Only it was not so much from you as from what you stood for," she hurried on. "I was thinking of myself alone, and of the present alone. I had been a prisoner so long, I wanted to be free a little."

"Free?" he broke in quickly, with a frown. "I don't like to hear you use that word. That's the way Covington's wife talked, is n't it?"

"Yes," she murmured.

"It's the way so many women are talking to-day—and so many men, too. Freedom is such a big word that a lot of people seem to think it will cloak anything they care to do. They lose sight of the fact that the freer a man or a woman is, the more responsibility he assumes. The free are put upon their honor to fulfill the obligations that are exacted by force from the irresponsible. So those who abuse this privilege are doubly treacherous—treacherous to themselves, and treacherous to society, which trusted them."

Marjory turned aside her head, so that he might not even look upon her with his blind eyes.

"I—I didn't mean any harm, Peter," she said.

"Of course you did n't. I don't suppose Mrs. Covington did, either; did she?"

"No, Peter, I'm sure she didn't. She—she was selfish."

"Besides, if you only come through safe, and learn—"

"At least, I've learned," she answered.

"Since you went away from me?"

"Yes."

"You have n't told me very much about that."

She caught her breath.

"Is—is it dishonest to keep to one's self how one learns?" she asked.

"No, little woman; only, I feel as though I'd like to know you as I know myself. I'd like to feel that there was n't a nook or cranny in your mind that was n't open to me."

"Peter!"

"Is that asking too much?"

"Some day you must know, but not now."

"If Mrs. Covington—"

"Must we talk any more about her?" she exclaimed.

"I did n't know it hurt you."

"It does—more than you realize."

"I'm sorry," he said quickly.

He fumbled about for her hand. She allowed him to take it.

"Have you heard from Covington since he left?"

He felt her fingers twitch.

"Does it hurt, too, to talk about him?" he asked.

"It's impossible to talk about Monte without talking about his—his—about Mrs. Covington," Marjory explained feebly.

"They ought to be one," he admitted. "But you said they are about to separate."

"Yes, Peter; only I keep thinking of what ought to be."

She withdrew her hand and leaned back on the seat a little away from him. Sensitive to every movement of hers, he glanced up at this.

"Somehow,"—he said, with a strained expression,—"somehow I feel the need of seeing your eyes to-day. There's something I 'm missing. There's something here I don't understand."

"Don't try to understand, Peter," she cried. "It's better that you should n't."

"It's best always to know the truth," he said.

"Not always."

"Always," he insisted.

"Sometimes it does n't do any good to know the truth. It only hurts."

"Even then, it's best. When I get my eyes—"

She shrank farther away from him, for she saw him struggling even then to open them.

It was this possibility which from that point on added a new terror to these daily drives. Marjory had told Monte that Peter's recovery was something to which she looked forward; but when she said that she had been sitting alone and pouring out her heart to Monte. She had not then been facing this fact by the side of Peter. It was one thing to dream boldly, with all her thoughts of Monte, and quite another to confront the same facts actually and alone. If this crisis came now, it was going to hurt her and hurt Peter, and do no good to any one; while, if it could be postponed six months, perhaps it would not hurt so much. It was better for Peter to endure his blindness a little longer than to see too soon. So the next day she decided she would not kiss his eyes. He came to her in the morning, and stood before her, waiting. She placed her hand upon his shoulder.

"Peter," she said as gently as she could, "I do not think I shall kiss you again for a little while."

She saw his lips tighten; but, to her surprise, he made no protest.

"No, dear heart," he answered.

"It is n't because I wish to be unkind," she said. "Only, until you know the whole truth, I don't feel honest with you."

"Come over by the window and sit down in the light," he requested.

With a start she glanced nervously at his eyes. They were closed. She took a chair in the sun, and he sat down opposite her.

For a moment they sat so, in silence. With her chin in her hand, she stared out across the blue waters of the Mediterranean, across the quay where Monte used to walk. It looked so desolate out there without him! How many hours since he left she had watched people pass back and forth along the broad path, as if hoping against hope that by some chance he might suddenly appear among them. But he never did, and she knew that she might sit here watching year after year and he would not come.

By this time he was probably in England—probably, on such a day as this, out upon the links. She smiled a little. "Damn golf!" he had said.

She thought for a moment that she heard his voice repeating it. It was only Peter's voice.

"You have grown even more beautiful than I thought," Peter was saying.

She sprang to her feet. He was looking at he—shading his opened eyes with one hand.

"Peter!" she cried, falling back a step.

"PETER!" SHE CRIED, FALLING BACK A STEP.

"Peter!" she cried, falling back a step.

"More beautiful," he repeated. "But your eyes are sadder."

"Peter," she said again, "your eyes are open!"

"Yes," he said. "It became necessary for me to see—so they opened."

Before them, she felt ashamed—almost like one naked. She began to tremble. Then, with her cheeks scarlet, she covered her face with her hands.

Peter rose and helped her back to a chair as if she, in her turn, had suddenly become blind.

"If I frighten you like this I—I must not look at you," he faltered.

Still she trembled; still she covered her face.

"See!" he cried. "I have closed them again."

She looked up in amazement. He was standing with his eyes tight shut. He who had been in darkness all these long months had dared, to save her from her own shame, to return again to the pit. For a second it stopped her heart from beating. Then, springing to his side, she seized his hands.

"Peter," she commanded, "open your eyes!"

He was pale—ghastly pale.

"Not if it hurts you."

Swiftly leaning toward him, she kissed the closed lids.

"Will you open them—now?"

She was in terror lest he should find it impossible again—as if that had been some temporary miracle which, having been scorned, would not be repeated.

Then once again she saw his eyes flutter open. This time she faced them with her fists clenched by her side. What a difference those eyes made in him. Closed, he was like a helpless child; open, he was a man. He grew taller, bigger, older, while she who had been leading him about shrank into insignificance. She felt pettier, plainer, less worthy than ever she had in her life. By sheer force of will power she held up her head and faced him as if she were facing the sun.

For a moment he feasted upon her hungrily. To see her hair, when for months he had been forced to content himself with memories of it; to see her white forehead, her big, deep eyes and straight nose; to see the lips which he had only felt—all that held him silent. But he saw something else there, too. In physical detail this face was the same that he had seen before he was stricken. But something had been added. Before she had the features of a girl; now she had the features of a woman. Something had since been added to the eyes and mouth—something he knew nothing about.

"Marjory," he said slowly, "I think there is a great deal you have left untold."

She tightened her lips. There was no further use of evasion. If he pressed her with his eyes open, he must know the truth.

"Yes, Peter," she answered.

"I can't decide," he went on slowly, "whether it has to do with a great grief or a great joy."

"The two so often come together," she trembled.

"Yes," he nodded; "I think that is true. Perhaps they belong together."

"I have only just learned that," she said.

"And you've been left with the grief?"

"I can't tell, Peter. Sometimes I think so, and then again I see the justice of it, and it seems beautiful. All I 'm sure of is that I 'm left alone."

"Even with me?"

"Even with you, Peter."

He passed his hand over his eyes.

"This other—do I know him?" he asked finally.

"Yes."

"It—it is Covington?"

"Yes."

She spoke almost mechanically.

"I—I should have guessed it before. Had I been able to see, I should have known."

"That is why I did n't wish you to see me—so soon," Marjory said.

"Covington!" he repeated. "But what of the other woman?"

She took a long breath.

"I—I'm the other woman," she answered.

"Marjory!" he cried. "Not she you told me of?"

"Yes."

"His wife!"

"No—not that. Merely Mrs. Covington."

"I don't understand. You don't mean you're not his wife!" He checked himself abruptly.

"We were married in Paris," she hastened to explain. "But—but we agreed the marriage was to be only a form. He was to come down here with me as a *compagnon de voyage*. He wished only to give me the protection of his name, and that—that was all I wished. It was not until I met you, Peter, that I realized what I had done."

"It was not until then you realized that you really loved him?"

"Not until then," she moaned.

"But, knowing that, you allowed me to talk as I did; to hope—"

"Peter—dear Peter!" she broke in. "It was not then. It was only after I knew he had gone out of my life forever that I allowed that. You see, he has gone. He has gone to England, and from there he is going home. You know what he is going for. He is never coming back. So it is as if he died, isn't it? I allowed you to talk because I knew you were telling the truth. And I did not promise much. When you asked me never to go from you, all I said was that I 'd try. You remember that? And I have tried, and I was going to keep on trying—ever so hard. I had ruined my own life and his life, and—and I did n't want to hurt you any more. I wanted to do what I could to undo some of the harm I'd already done. I thought that perhaps if we went on like this long enough, I might forget a little of the past and look forward only to the future. Some day I meant to tell you. You know that, Peter. You know I would n't be dishonest with you." She was talking hysterically, anxious only to relieve the tenseness of his lips. She was not sure that he heard her at all. He was looking at her, but with curious detachment, as if he were at a play.

"Peter—say something!" she begged.

"It's extraordinary that I should ever have dared hope you were for me," he said.

"You mean you—you don't want me, Peter?"

"Want you?" he cried hoarsely. "I'd go through hell to get you. I'd stay mole-blind the rest of my life to get you! Want you?"

He stepped toward her with his hands outstretched as if to seize her. In spite of herself, she shrank away.

"You see," he ran on. "What difference does it make if I want you? You belong to another. You belong to Covington. You have n't anything to do with yourself any more. You have n't yourself to give. You're his."

With her hand above her eyes as if to ward off his blows, she gasped:—

"You must n't say such things, Peter."

"I'm only telling the truth, and there's no harm in that. I 'm telling you what you have n't dared tell yourself."

"Things I mustn't tell myself!" she cried. "Things I must n't hear."

"What I don't understand," he said, "is why Covington did n't tell you all this himself. He must have known."

"He knew nothing," she broke in. "I was a mere incident in his life. We met in Paris quite by accident when he happened to have an idle week. He was alone and I was alone, and he saved me from a disagreeable situation. Then, because he still had nothing in particular to do and I had nothing in particular to do, he suggested this further arrangement. We were each considering nothing but our own comfort. We wanted nothing more. It was to escape just such complications as this—to escape responsibility, as I told you—that we—we married. He was only a boy, Peter, and knew no better. But I was a woman, and should have known. And I came to know! That was my punishment."

"He came to know, too," said Peter.

"He might have come to know," she corrected breathlessly. "There were moments when I dared think so. If I had kept myself true—oh, Peter, these are terrible things to say!"

She buried her face in her hands again—a picture of total and abject misery. Her frame shook with sobs that she was fighting hard to suppress.

Peter placed his hand gently upon her shoulder.

"There, little woman," he tried to comfort. "Cry a minute. It will do you good."

"I have n't even the right to cry," she sobbed.

"You *must* cry," he said. "You have n't let yourself go enough. That's been the whole trouble."

He was silent a moment, patting her back, with his eyes leveled out of the window as if trying to look beyond the horizon, beyond that to the secret places of eternity.

"You have n't let yourself go enough," he repeated, almost like a seer. "You have tried to force your destiny from its appointed course. You have, and Covington has, and I have. We have tried to force things that were not meant to be and to balk things that were meant to be. That's because we've been selfish—all three of us. We've each thought of ourself alone—of our own petty little happiness of the moment. That's deadly. It warps the vision. It—it makes people stone-blind.

"I understand now. When you went away from me, it was myself alone I considered. I was hurt and worried, and made a martyr of myself. If I had thought more of you, all would have been well. This time I think I—I have thought a little more of you. It was to get at you and not myself that I wanted to see again. So I saw again. I let go of myself and reached out for you. So now—why, everything is quite clear."

She raised her head.

"Clear, Peter?"

"Quite clear. I'm to go back to my work, and to use my eyes less and my head and heart more. I 'm to deal less with statutes and more with people. Instead of quoting precedents, perhaps I 'm going to try to establish precedents. There's work enough to be done, God knows, of a sort that is born of just such a year as this I 've lived through. I must let go of myself and let myself go. I must think less of my own ambitions and more of the ambitions of others. So I shall live in others. Perhaps I may even be able to live a little through you two."

"Peter!" she cried.

"For Covington must come back to you as fast as ever he can."

"No! No! No!"

"You don't understand how much he loves his wife."

"Please!"

"And, he, poor devil, does n't understand how much his wife loves him."

"You—you"—she trembled aghast—"you would n't dare repeat what I've told you!"

"You don't want to stagger on in the dark any longer. You'll let me tell him."

She rose to her feet, her face white.

"Peter," she said slowly, "if ever you told him that, I'd never forgive you. If ever you told him, I 'd deny it. You 'd only force me into more lies. You'd only crush me lower."

"Steady, Marjory," he said.

"You're wonderful, Peter!" she exclaimed. "You 've—you 've been seeing visions. But when you speak of telling him what I've told you, you don't understand how terrible that would be. Peter—you'll promise me you won't do that?"

She was pleading, with panic in her eyes.

"Yet, if he knew, he'd come racing to you."

"He'd do that because he's a gentleman and four-square. He'd come to me and pretend. He'd feel himself at fault, and pity me. Do you know how it hurts a woman to be pitied? I'd rather he'd hate me. I'd rather he'd forget me altogether.",

"But what of the talks I had with him in the dark?" he questioned. "When he talked to me of you then, it was not in pity."

"Because,"—she choked,—"because he does n't know himself as I know him. He—he does n't like changes—dear Monte. It disturbed him to go because it would have been so much easier to have stayed. So, for the moment, he may have been—a bit sentimental."

"You don't think as little of him as that!" he cried.

"He—he is the man who married me," she answered unsteadily. "It was—just Monte who married me—honest, easy-going, care-free Monte, who is willing to do a woman a favor even to the extent of marrying her. He is very honest and very gallant and very normal. He likes one day to be as another. He does n't wish to be stirred up. He asked me this, Peter: 'Is n't it possible to care without caring too much?' And I said, 'Yes.' That was why he married me. He had seen others who cared a great deal, and they frightened him. They cared so much that they made themselves uncomfortable, and he feared that."

"Good Lord, you call that man Covington?" exclaimed Peter.

"No—just Monte," Marjory answered quickly. "It's just the outside of him. The man you call Covington—the man inside—is another man."

"It's the real man," declared Peter.

"Yes," she nodded, with a catch in her voice. "That's the real man. But—don't you understand?—it was n't that man who married me. It was Monte who married me to escape Covington. He trusted me not to disturb the real man, just as I trusted him not to disturb the real me."

Peter leaned forward with a new hope in his eyes.

"Then," he said, "perhaps, after all, he did n't get to the real you."

Quite simply she replied:—

"He did, Peter. He does not know it, but he did."

"You are sure?"

She knew the pain she was causing him, but she answered:—

"Yes. I could n't admit that to any one else in the world but you—and it hurts you, Peter."

"It hurts like the devil," he said.

She placed her hand upon his.

"Poor Peter," she said gently.

"It hurts like the devil, but it's nothing for you to pity me for," he put in quickly. "I'd rather have the hurt from you than nothing."

"You feel like that?" she asked earnestly.

"Yes."

"Then," she said, "you must understand how, even with me, the joy and the grief are one?"

"Yes, I understand that. Only if he knew—"

"He'd come back to me, you're going to say again. And I tell you again, I won't have him come back, kind and gentle and smiling. If he came back now,—if it were possible for him really to come to me,—I'd want him to ache with love. I'd want him to be hurt with love."

She was talking fiercely, with a wild, unrestrained passion such as Peter had never seen in any woman.

"I'd want," she hurried on, out of all control of herself—"I'd want everything I don't want him to give—everything I've no right to ask. I'd want him to live on tiptoe from one morning through to the next. I'd begrudge him every minute he was just comfortable. I'd want him always eager, always worried, because I'd be always looking for him to do great things. I'd have him always ready for great sacrifices—not for me alone, but for himself. I'd be so proud of him I think I—I could with a smile see him sacrifice even his life for another. For I should know that, after a little waiting, I should meet him again, a finer and nobler man. And all those things I asked of him I should want to do for him. I'd like to lay down my life for him."

She stopped as abruptly as she had begun, staring about like some one suddenly awakened to find herself in a strange country. It was Peter's voice that brought her back again to the empty room.

"How you do love him!" he said solemnly.

"Peter," she cried, "you shouldn't have listened!"

She shrank back toward the door.

"And I—I thought just kisses on the eyes stood for love," he added.

"You must forget all I said," she moaned. "I was mad—for a moment!"

"You were wonderful," he told her.

She was still backing toward the door.

"I'm going off to hide," she said piteously.

"Not that," he called after her.

But the door closed in front of her. The door closed in front of him. With his lips clenched, Peter Noyes walked back to the Hôtel des Roses.

CHAPTER XXV
SO LONG

When Peter stepped into his sister's room he had forgotten that his eyes were open.

"Beatrice," he said, "we must start back for New York as soon as possible."

She sprang from her chair. Pale and without his shade, he was like an apparition.

"Peter!" she cried.

"What's the trouble?"

"Your eyes!"

"They came back this morning."

"Then I was right! Marjory—Marjory worked the miracle!"

He smiled a little.

"Yes."

"It's wonderful. But, Peter—"

"Well?"

"You look so strange—so pale!"

"It's been—well, rather an exciting experience."

She put her arms about his neck and kissed him.

"You should have brought the miracle-worker with you," she smiled.

"And instead of that I'm leaving her."

"Leaving Marjory—after this?"

"Sit down, little sister," he begged. "A great deal has happened this morning—a great deal that I'm afraid it's going to be hard for you to understand. It was hard for me to understand at first; and yet, after all, it's merely a question of fact. It is n't anything that leaves any chance for speculation. It just is, that's all. You see, you—both of us—made an extraordinary mistake. We—we assumed that Marjory was free."

"Free? Of course she's free!" exclaimed Beatrice.

"Only she's not," Peter informed her. "As a matter of fact, she's married."

"Marjory—married!"

"To Covington. She's Covington's wife. They were married a few weeks ago in Paris. You understand? She's Covington's wife." His voice rose a trifle.

"Peter—you're sure of that?"

"She told me so herself—less than an hour ago."

"That's impossible. Why, she listened to me when—"

"When what?" he cut in.

Frightened, she clasped her hands beneath her chin.

His eyes demanded a reply.

"I—I told her what the doctors told me. Don't look at me so, Peter!"

"You tried to win her sympathy for me?"

"They told me if you stopped worrying, your sight would come back. I told her that, Peter."

"You told her more?"

"That if she could love you—oh, I could n't help it!"

"So that is why she listened to you; why she listened to me. You begged for her pity, and—she gave it. I thought at least I could leave her with my head up."

Beatrice began to sob.

"I—I did the best I knew how," she pleaded.

His head was bowed. He looked crushed. Throwing herself upon her knees in front of him, Beatrice reached for his clasped hands.

"I did the best I knew!" she moaned.

"Yes," he answered dully; "you did that. Every one has done that. Only—nothing should have been done at all. Nothing can ever be done."

"You—you forgive me, Peter?"

"Yes."

But his voice was dead. It had no meaning.

"It may all be for the best," she ran on, anxious to revive him. "We'll go back to New York, Peter—you and I. Perhaps you'll let me stay with you there. We'll get a little apartment together, so that I can care for you. I'll do that all the days of my life, if you'll let me."

"I want a better fate than that for you, little sister," he answered.

Rising, he helped her to her feet. He smoothed back her hair from her forehead and kissed her there.

"It won't do to look ahead very far, or backwards either just now," he said. "But if I can believe there is something still left in life for me, I must believe there is a great deal more left for you. Only we must get away from here as soon as possible."

"You have your eyes, Peter," she exclaimed exultingly. "She can't take those away from you again!"

"Hush," he warned. "You must never blame her for anything."

"You mean you still—"

"Still and forever, little sister," he answered. "But we must not talk of that."

"Poor Peter," she trembled.

"Rich Peter!" he corrected, with a wan smile. "There are so many who have n't as much as that."

He went back to his room. The next thing to do was to write some sort of explanation to Covington. His ears burned as he thought of the other letter he had sent. How it must have bored into the man! How it must have hurt! He had been forced to read the confession of love of another man for his wife. The wonder was that he had not taken the next train back and knocked down the writer. It must be that he understood the hopelessness of such a passion. Perhaps he had smiled! Only that was not like Covington. Rather, he had gripped his jaws and stood it.

But if it had hurt and he hankered for revenge, he was to have it now. He, Noyes, had bared his soul to the husband and confessed a love that now he must stand up and recant. That was punishment enough for any man. He must do that, too, without violating any of Marjory's confidences—without helping in any way to disentangle the pitiful snarl that it was within his power to disentangle. She whose happiness might partly have recompensed him for what he had to do, he must still leave unhappy. As far as he himself was concerned, however, he was entitled to tell the truth. He could not recant his love. That would be false. But he had no right to it—that was what he must make Covington understand.

Dear Covington [he began]: I am writing this with my eyes open. The miracle I spoke of came to pass. Also a great many other things have come to pass. You'll realize how hard it is to write about them after that other letter, when

I tell you I have learned the truth: that Marjory is Mrs. Covington. She told me herself, when our relations reached a crisis where she had to tell.

I feel, naturally, as if I owed you some sort of apology; and yet, when I come to frame it, I find myself baffled. Of course I'm leaving for home as soon as possible—probably to-morrow. Of course if I had known the truth I should have left long ago, and that letter would never have had any occasion for being written. I'm assuming, Covington, that you will believe that without any question. You knew what I did not know and did not tell me even after you knew how I felt. I suppose you felt so confident of her that you trusted her absolutely to handle an affair of this sort herself.

I want to say right here, you were justified. Whatever in that other letter I may have said to lead you to believe she had come to care for me in the slightest was a result solely of my own self-delusion and her innate gentleness. I have discovered that my sister, meaning no harm, went to her and told her that the restoration of my sight depended upon her interest in me. It was manifestly unfair of my sister to put it that way, but the little woman was thinking only of me. I'm sorry it was done. Evidently it was the basis upon which she made the feeble promise I spoke of, and which I exaggerated into something more.

She cared for me no more than for a friend temporarily afflicted. That's all, Covington. Neither in word nor thought nor deed has she ever gone any further. Looking back upon the last few days now, it is clear enough. Rather than hurt me, she allowed me to talk—allowed me to believe. Rather, she suffered it. It was not pleasant for her. She endured it because of what my sister had said. It seems hard luck that I should have been led in this fashion to add to whatever other burdens she may have had.

I ask you to believe—it would be an impertinence, except for what I told you before—that on her side there has been nothing between us of which you could not approve.

Now for myself. In the light of what I know to-day, I could not have written you of her as I did. Yet, had I remained silent, all I said would have remained just as much God's truth as then. Though I must admit the utter hopelessness of my love, I see no reason why I should think of attempting to deny that love. It would n't be decent to myself, to you, or to her. It began before you came into her life at all. It has grown bigger and cleaner since then. It persists to-day. I'm talking to you as man to man, Covington. I know you won't confuse that statement with any desire on my part—with any hope, however remote—to see that love fulfilled further than it is fulfilled to-day. That delusion has vanished forever. I shall never entertain it again, no matter what course your destiny or her destiny may take. I cannot make that emphatic enough, Covington. It is based upon a certain knowledge of facts which, unfortunately, I am not at liberty to reveal to you.

So, as far as my own emotions are concerned then, I retract nothing of what I told you. In fact, to-day I could say more. To me she is and ever will be the most wonderful woman who ever lived. Thinking of you before, I said there ought to be two of her, so that one might be left for you. Now, thinking of myself, I would to God there were two of her, so that one might be left for me. Yet that is inconceivable. It might be possible to find another who looked like her; who thought like her; who was willing for the big things of life like her. But this other would not be Marjory. Besides everything else she has in common with other women, she has something all her own that makes her herself. It's that something that has got hold of me, Covington.

I don't suppose it's in particularly good taste for me to talk to you of your wife in this fashion; but it's my dying speech, old man, as far as this subject is concerned, and I'm talking to you and to no one else.

There's just one thing more I want to say. I don't want either you or Marjory to think I'm going out of your lives a martyr—that I'm going off to pine and die. The first time she left me I made an ass of myself, and that was because I had not then got hold of the essential fact of love. As I see it now, love—real love—does not lie in the personal gratification of selfish desires. The wanting is only the first stage. Perhaps it is a ruse of Nature to entice men to the second stage, which is giving.

Until recently my whole thought was centered on getting. I was thinking of myself alone. It was baffled desire and injured vanity that led me to do what I did before, and I was justly punished. It was when I began to think less about myself and more about her that I was reprieved. I'm leaving her now with but one desire: to do for her whatever I may, at any time and in any place, to make her happy; and, because of her, to do the same for any others with whom for the rest of my life I may be thrown in contact. Thus I may be of some use and find peace.

I'm going away, Covington. That will leave her here alone. Wherever you are, there must be trains back to Nice—starting perhaps within the hour.

So long.

PETER J. NOYES.

CHAPTER XXVI
FREEDOM

With the departure of Peter and his sister—Peter had made his leave-taking easy by securing an earlier train than she had expected and sending her a brief note of farewell—Marjory found herself near that ideal state of perfect freedom she had craved. There was now no outside influence to check her movements. If she remained where she was, there was no one to interrupt her in the solitary pursuit of her own pleasure. Safe from any possibility of intrusion, she was at liberty to remain in the seclusion of her room; but, if she preferred, she could walk the quay without the slightest prospect in the world of being forced to recognize the friendly greeting of any one.

Peter was gone; Beatrice was gone; and Monte was gone. There was no one else—unless by some chance poor Teddy Hamilton should turn up, which was so unlikely that she did not even consider it. Yet there were moments when, if she had met Teddy, she would have smiled a welcome. She would not have feared him. There was only one person in the world now of whom she stood in fear, and he was somewhere along the English coast, playing a poor game of golf.

She was free beyond her most extravagant dreams—absolutely free. She was so free that it seemed aimless to rise in the morning, because there was nothing awaiting her attention. She was so free that there was no object in breakfasting, because there was no obligation demanding her strength. She was so free that whether she should go out or remain indoors depended merely upon the whim of the moment. There was for her nothing either without or within.

For the first twenty-four hours she sat in a sort of stupor.

Marie became anxious.

"Madame is not well?" she asked solicitously.

"Perfectly well," answered Marjory dully.

"Madame's cheeks are very white," Marie ventured further.

Madame shrugged her shoulders.

"Is there any harm in that?" she demanded.

"It is such a beautiful day to walk," suggested Marie.

Marjory turned slowly.

"What do you mean by beautiful?"

"Ma foi, the sky is blue, the sun is shining, the birds singing," explained Marie.

"Do those things make a beautiful day?"

"What else, madame?" inquired the maid, in astonishment.

"I do not know," sighed madame. "All I know is that for me those things do not count at all."

"Then," declared Marie, "it is time to call a doctor."

"For what?"

"To make madame see the blue sky again and hear the birds."

"But I do not care whether I see them or not," concluded madame, turning away from the subject.

Here was the whole thing in a nutshell. There were some who might consider this to be an ideal state. Not to care about anything at all was not to have anything at all to worry about. Certain philosophies were based upon this state of mind. In part, Monte's own philosophy was so based. If not to care too much were well, then not to care at all should be better. It should leave one utterly and sublimely free. But should it also leave one utterly miserable?

There was something inconsistent in that—something unfair. To be free, and yet to feel like a prisoner bound and gagged; not to care, and yet to feel one's vitals eaten with caring; to obtain one's objective, and then to be marooned there like a forsaken sailor on a desert island—this was unjust.

Ah, but she did care! It was as if some portion of her refused absolutely to obey her will in this matter. In silence she might declare her determination not to care, or through tense lips she might mutter the same thing in spoken words; but this made no difference. She was a free agent, to be sure. She had the right to dictate terms to herself. She had the sole right to be arbiter of her destiny. It was to that end she had craved freedom. It was for her alone to decide about what she should care and should not care. She was no longer a schoolgirl to be controlled by others. She was both judge and jury for herself, and she had passed sentence to the effect that, since she had chosen not to care when to care had been her privilege, it was no longer her privilege to care when she chose to care. Nothing since then had developed to give her the right to alter that verdict. If anything, it held truer after Peter's departure than ever. She must add to her indictment the harm she had done him.

Still, she cared. Staring out of her window upon the quay, she caught her breath at sight of every new passer-by, in fearful hope that it might prove to be Monte. She did this when she knew that Monte was hundreds of miles away. She did this in face of the fact that, if his coming depended upon her consent, she would have withheld that consent. If in truth he had suddenly appeared, she would have fled in terror. He must not come; he should not come—but, O God, if he would come!

"But, O God, if he would come!"

Sometimes this thought held her for a moment before she realized it. Then for a space the sun appeared in the blue sky and the birds set up such a singing as Marie had never heard in all her life. Perhaps for a step or two she saw him striding toward her with his face aglow, his clear, blue eyes smiling, his tender man mouth open to greet her. So her heart leaped to her throat and her arms trembled. Then—the fall into the abyss as she caught herself. Then her head drooping upon her arm and the racking, dry sobs.

How she did care! It was as if everything she had ever hungered for in the past—all her beautiful, timid girlhood dreams; all that good part of her later hunger for freedom; all of to-day and all that was worth while of the days to come, had been gathered together, like jewels in a single jewel casket, and handed over to him. He had them all. None had been left her. She had none left.

She had always known that if ever she loved it was so that she must love. It was this that she had feared. She had known that if she gave at all she must give utterly—all that she ever had or hoped to have. Suddenly she recalled

Mrs. Chic. It was with a new emotion. The latter had always been to her the symbol of complete self-sacrifice. It centered around the night Chic, Junior was born. That night she had been paler than Mrs. Chic herself; she had whimpered more than Mrs. Chic. Outside, waiting, she had feared more than the wife within who was wrestling with death for a new life. She had sat alone, with her hands over her ears in an agony of fear and horror. She had marveled that any woman would consent to face such a crisis. It had seemed wrong that love—an affair of orange blossoms and music and laughter—should lead to that. Wide-eyed, she had sobbed in terror until it was over. It was with awe and wonder that a few days later she had seen Mrs. Chic lying in her big white bed so croonigly happy and jubilant.

Now she understood. The fear and horror had vanished. Had she been in the next room to-day, her heart would have leaped with joy in tune with her who was fighting her grim fight. Because the aches and the pains are but an incident of preparation. Not only that, but one can so love that pain, physical pain, may in the end be the only means for an adequate expression of that love. The two may be one, so blended as to lead, in the end, to perfect joy. Even mental pains, such as she herself now suffered, can do that. For all she was undergoing she would not have given up one second to be back again where she was a month before.

Something comes with love. It is that more than love itself which is the greatest thing in the world. Sitting by her window, watching the shadows pass, Marjory was sensing this. The knowledge was coming slowly, imperceptibly; but it was bringing her strength. It was steadying her nerves. It was preparing her for the supreme test.

Because that very day, toward sunset-time, as she still sat by her window, she saw a shadow that looked like Monte. She smiled a little, because she knew it would soon dissolve. Rapidly the shadow strode along the quay until opposite the hotel. Then, instead of vanishing, it came on—straight toward her. She sprang to her feet, leaning back against the wall, not daring to look again. So she stood, counting her heart-beats; for she was still certain that when a hundred or so of them had passed, the illusion also would fade.

Marjory did not have time to count a full hundred heart-beats before she heard a light rap at the door. For the fraction of a second she swayed in the fear that, taking the stairs three at a time, Monte might have ventured to her very room. But it would be with no such gentle tap that he would announce himself.

"Yes?" she called.

"A card for madame," came the voice of the garçon.

Her knees still weak, she crossed the room and took the card. There was no longer any hope left to her. Apparitions do not materialize to the point where they present their cards.

"Madame is in?" queried the boy.

"What else can I say?" she asked, as if, in her desperate need, seeking counsel of him.

The boy shrugged his shoulders.

"If madame desires, I can report madame is away," he offered.

It was all one to him. It was all one to every one else in the world but herself. No one was interested. She was alone. Then why had not Monte himself let her alone? That was the point, but to determine that it was necessary to see him.

It was possible he had come merely by chance. It was possible he had come to see Peter, not knowing that Peter had gone. It was possible he had returned this way in order to take the Mediterranean route home. On the face of it, anything was more probable than that he had come deliberately to see her.

"You will ask monsieur to wait, and I will be down in a few moments," she replied to the boy.

She called to Marie.

"I have a caller," she announced nervously. "You must make me look as young as possible."

Even if she had grown old inside, there was no reason why she should reveal her secret.

"I am glad," nodded Marie. "Madame should put on a white gown and wear a ribbon in her hair."

"A ribbon!" exclaimed madame. "That would look absurd."

"You shall see."

She was too weak to protest. She was glad enough to sit down and give herself up utterly to Marie.

"Only we must not keep him waiting too long," she said. "Monsieur Covington does not like to be kept waiting."

"It is he?" exclaimed Marie.

"It—it is quite a surprise." She blushed. "I—I do not understand why he is here."

"It should not be difficult to understand," ventured Marie.

To that madame made no reply. It was clear enough what Marie meant. It was a natural enough mistake. To her, Monsieur Covington was still the husband of madame. She had stood in the little chapel in Paris when madame was married. When one was married, one was married; and that was all there was to it for all time. So, doubtless, Marie reasoned. It was the simple peasant way—the old, honest, woman way.

Madame folded her hands in her lap and closed her eyes while Marie did her hair and adjusted the ribbon. Then Marie slipped a white gown over her head.

"There," concluded the maid, with satisfaction, as she fastened the last hook. "Madame looks as young as when she was married."

But the color that made her look young vanished the moment Marjory started down the stairs alone to meet him. Several times she paused to catch her breath; several times she was upon the point of turning back. Then she saw him coming up to meet her. She felt her hand in his.

"Jove!" he was saying, "but it's good to see you again."

"But I don't understand why you are here," she managed to gasp.

To him it was evidently as simple as to Marie.

"To see you," he answered promptly.

"If that is all, then you should not have come," she declared.

They were still on the stairs. She led the way down and into the lower reception-room. She did not care to go again into the sun parlor. She thought it would be easier to talk to him in surroundings not associated with anything in the past. They had the room to themselves. She sat down and motioned him to another chair at some little distance. He paid no attention to her implied request. With his feet planted firmly, his arms folded, he stood before her while she tried to find some way of avoiding his gaze.

"Peter Noyes has gone," he began.

"Yes," she nodded. "You heard about his eyes?"

"He wrote me."

She looked up swiftly.

"Peter wrote you?" she trembled.

"He told me he had recovered his sight. He told me he was going."

What else had he told? Dizzily she waited. For the first time in her life, she felt as if she might faint. That would be such a silly thing to do!

"He said he was going home—out of your life."

Peter had told Monte that! What else had he told?

He paused a moment, as if expecting her to make some reply. There, was nothing she could say.

"It was n't what I expected," he went on.

What else had Peter told him?

"Was n't there any other way?" he asked.

"I did n't send him home. He—he chose to go," she said.

"Because it was n't any use for him to remain?"

"I told him the truth," she nodded.

"And he took it like a man!" exclaimed Monte enthusiastically. "I 'd like to show you his letter, only I don't know that it would be quite fair to him."

"I don't want to see it," she cut in. "I—I know I should n't."

What else besides his going had Peter told Monte?

"It was his letter that brought me back," he said.

She held her breath. She had warned Peter that if he as much as hinted at anything that she had confessed to him, she would lie to Monte. So she should—but God forbid that this added humiliation be brought upon her.

"You see, when I went I expected that he would be left to care for you. With him and his sister here, I knew you would n't be alone. I thought they'd stay, or if they went—you'd go with them."

"But why should n't I be alone?" she gathered strength to ask.

"Because," he answered quickly, "it is n't good for you. It is n't good for any one. Besides, it is n't right. When we were married I made certain promises, and those hold good until we're unmarried."

"Monte!" she cried.

"As long as Peter was around, that was one thing; now that he's gone—"

"It throws me back on your hands," she interrupted, in an attempt to assert herself. "Please to sit down. You're making your old mistake of trying to be serious. There's not the slightest reason in the world why you should bother about me like this."

She ventured to look at him again. His brows were drawn together in a puzzled frown. Dear Monte—it was cruel of her to confuse him like this, when he was trying to see straight. He looked so very woe-begone when he looked troubled at all.

"It—it is n't any bother," he stammered.

"I should think it was a good deal," she answered, feeling for a moment that she had the upper hand. "Where did you come from to here?"

"Paris."

"You did n't go on to England at all?"

"No."

"Then you did n't get back to your schedule. If you had done that, you would n't have had any time left to—to think about other things."

"I did n't get beyond the Normandie," he answered. "My schedule stopped short right there."

He was still standing before her. Apparently he intended to remain. So she rose and crossed to another chair. He followed.

"You should have gone on," she insisted.

"I had my old room—next to yours," he said.

She must trouble him still more. There was no other way.

"That was rather sentimental of you, Monte, was n't it?" she asked lightly.

"I went there as a man goes home," he answered softly.

Her lips became suddenly dumb.

"Then I had a long letter from Peter; the first one."

"He has written you before?"

"He wrote me that he loved you and was going to marry you. That was before he learned the truth."

"About you?"

"And about you. When he wrote again, he said you had told him everything."

So she had; more, far more than she should. What of that had he told Monte? The question left her faint again.

"How did it happen?" he asked.

"I—I don't know," she faltered. "He guessed a little, and then I had to tell him the rest."

Monte's mouth hardened.

"That should n't have been left for you to do. I should have told him myself."

"Now that it's all over—can't we forget it, Monte, with all the rest?"

He bent a little toward her.

"Have you forgotten all the rest?" he demanded.

"At least, I 'm trying," she gasped.

"I wonder if you have found it as hard as I even to try?"

Steady—she must hold herself steady. His words were afire. With her eyes on the ground, she felt his eyes searching her face.

"Whether it is hard or not makes no difference," she answered.

"It's just that which makes all the difference in the world," he contradicted. "I wanted to be honest with myself and with you. So I went away, willing to forget if that were the honest way. But, from the moment I took the train here at Nice, I've done nothing but remember. I've remembered every single minute of the time since I met you in Paris. The present has been made up of nothing but the past. Passing hours were nothing but echoes of past hours.

"I've remembered everything—even things away back that I thought I had forgotten. I dug up even those glimpses I had had of you at Chic's house when you were only a school-girl. And I did n't do it on purpose, Marjory. I 'd have been glad not to do it, because at the time it hurt to remember them. I thought I'd given you over to Peter. I thought he was going to take you away from me. So I 'd have been glad enough to forget, if it had been possible."

She sprang to her feet.

"What are you saying, Monte?" she trembled.

With his head erect and his eyes shining, he was telling her what her heart hungered to hear. That was what he was doing. Only she must not listen.

"I'm telling you that to forget was not possible," he repeated hotly; "I'm telling you that I shall never try again. I've come back to get you and keep you this time."

He held out his arms to her. She shrank back.

"You're making it so hard," she quavered.

"Come to me," he said gently. "That's the easy way. I love you, Marjory. Don't you understand? I love you with all my heart and soul, and I want you to begin life with me now in earnest. Come, little woman."

He reached her hands and tried to draw her toward him. She resisted with all her strength.

"You must n't," she gasped. "You must n't!"

"It's you who're making it hard now, wife o' mine," he whispered.

Yes, she was making it hard. But she must make it still harder. He had come back to her because she was alone, moved temporarily by a feeling of sentimental responsibility. That was all. He was sincere enough for the moment, but she must not confuse this with any deeper passion. He had made a mistake in returning to the Normandie. Doubtless he had felt lonesome there. It was only natural that he should exaggerate that, for the time being, into something more.

Then Peter's two letters had come. If Peter had not told him anything that he should n't, he had probably told him a great deal more than he should. Monte, big-hearted and good, had, as a consequence of all these things, imagined himself in love. This delusion might last a week or two; and then, when he came to himself again, the rude awakening would follow. He would see her then merely as a trifler. Worse than that, he might see himself as merely a trifler. That would be deadly.

"It's you who are making it hard now," he repeated.

She had succeeded in freeing herself, leaving him before her as amazed and hurt as a spurned child.

"You're forcing me to run away from you—to run away as I did from the others," she said.

He staggered before the blow.

"Not that!" he cried hoarsely.

"I'm going home," she ran on. "I'm going back to my little farm, where I started."

"You're running away—from me?"

"I must go right off."

She looked around as if for Marie. It was as if she were about to start that second.

"Where is Marie?" she asked dully.

She made for the door.

"Marjory," he called after her. "Don't do that!"

"I must go—right off," she said again.

"Wife o' mine," he cried, "there is no need of that."

"Marie!" she called as she reached the door. "Marie!" Frantically she ran up the stairs.

CHAPTER XXVII
WAR

War!

A summer sky, warm and fragrant, suddenly became dour and overcast. Within a day thunder rolled and lightning flashed. Men glanced up in startled surprise, then clenched their jaws. Women who were laughing gayly turned suddenly white. Orders were speeded over the wires and through the clouds to the remotest hamlets of France. In a few hours men began to gather in uniform, bearing rifles. They posted themselves about the gates of stations. They increased in numbers until they were everywhere. Trumpets sounded, drums rolled. Excited groups gathered in the hotels and rushed off to the consulates. The very air was tense and vibrant.

War!

People massed in groups. The individual no longer counted. Storekeepers, bankers, dandies, chauffeurs, postmen, gardeners, hotel proprietors became merely Frenchmen. They dropped the clothes that distinguished their caste, and became merely men in uniform.

Foreign visitors no longer counted as individuals. They ran about in panic-stricken groups like vagrant dogs. Those in uniform looked on indifferently, or gave sharp orders turning strangers back from this road or that, this gate or that. A chauffeur in uniform might turn back his millionaire foreign master.

Credit money no longer counted. Banks refused to give out gold, and the shopkeepers and hotel proprietors refused to accept anything but gold. No one knew what might happen, and refused to risk. A man might brandish a letter of credit for ten thousand francs and be refused a glass of wine. A man with a thousand francs in gold was in a better position than a millionaire with only paper.

Monte discovered this when he hurried to his own bankers. With half a million dollars and more to his credit at home, he was not allowed a single louis d'or. Somewhat bewildered, he stood on the steps and counted the gold he happened to have in his pockets. It amounted to some fifty dollars. To all intents and purposes, that embraced his entire capital. In the present emergency his stocks and bonds were of no avail whatever to him. He thought of the cables, but gold could not be cabled—only more credit, which in this grim crisis went for nothing. It was as if he had suddenly been forced into bankruptcy. His fortune temporarily had been swept away.

If that was true of his own, it must be equally true of Marjory's. She was no wealthier now than the sum total of the gold she happened to have in her possession. The thought came to him at first as a shock. What was she going to do? She was upon the point of leaving, and her plans must have been suddenly checked. She was, in effect, a prisoner here. She was stranded as completely as if she were any penniless young woman.

Then some emotion—some feeling indistinctly connected with the grandfather who had crossed the plains in forty-nine—swept over him. It was a primitive exultation. It made him conscious of the muscles in his back and legs. It made him throw back his head and square his shoulders. A moment before, with railroads and steamships at her command, with a hundred men standing ready to do her bidding in response to the magic of her check-book, she had been as much mistress of her little world as any ancient queen.

Sweaty men were rushing fruits from the tropics, silks from India, diamonds from Africa, caviar from the north; others were making ready fine quarters in every corner of the globe; others were weaving cloths and making shoes; others were rehearsing plays and music—all for her and others like her, who had only to call upon their banks to pay for all this toil. Instead of one man to supply her needs, she had a thousand, ten thousand. With the machinery of civilization working smoothly, she had only to nod—and sign a check.

Now, overnight, this had been changed. The machinery was to be put to other uses. Ships that had been carrying silks were needed for men with rifles. Railroads were for troops. The sweat of men was to be in battle. Servants were to be used for the slaughter of other servants. With nations at one another's throats, the very basis of credit, mutual trust and esteem, was gone. She and others like her did not count. Men with the lust for blood in their hearts could not bother with them. They might sit in their rooms and sob, or they might starve. It did not much matter. A check was only a bit of paper. Under such conditions it might be good or not. Gold was what counted—gold and men. Broad backs counted, and stout legs.

Monte took a deep breath. Now—it might be possible that he would count. It was so that his grandfather had counted. He had fought his way across a continent and back for just such another woman as Marjory. Life had been primitive then. It was primitive now. Men and women were forced to stand together and take the long road side by side.

The blood rushed to Monte's head. He must get to her at once. She would need him now—if only for a little while. He must carry her home. She could not go without him.

He started down the steps of the bank, two at a time, and almost ran against her. She was on her way to the bank as he had been, in search of gold. Her eyes greeted him with the welcome her lips would not.

"You see!" he exclaimed, with a quick laugh.

"When you need me I come."

She was dressed in the very traveling costume she had worn when they left Paris together. She was wearing, too, the same hat. It might have been yesterday.

"They refused my check at the hotel," she explained nervously. "They say they must have gold."

"Have you any?" he asked.

"One louis d'or."

"And I have ten," he informed her.

She did not understand why he should be so exultant over this fact.

"I have come here to get enough to pay my bill and buy my ticket. I am leaving this morning."

"They won't give you any," he explained. "Besides, they won't carry you on the train unless you put on a uniform."

"Monte!"

"It's a fact."

"Then—what am I to do?"

She looked quite helpless—deliciously helpless.

He laughed joyously.

"You are bankrupt," he said. "So am I. We have only fifty-five dollars between us. But that is something. Also there is the machine. That will take us over the Italian frontier and to Genoa. I ought to be able to sell it there for something. Come on."

"Where?" she asked.

"We must get the car as soon as possible. I have a notion that with every passing hour it is going to be more difficult to get out."

"But I'm not going with you, Monte. It's—it's impossible!"

"It's the only way, little woman."

He gave her no time to argue about it, but took her arm and hurried her to the garage. It was necessary to walk. Taxis were as if they had never been. They passed groups of soldiers who turned to look at Marjory. The eyes of many were hot with wine, and she was very glad that she was not alone.

At the door of the garage stood a soldier in uniform. As Monte attempted to pass, he was brought to a halt.

"It is not permitted to pass," explained the guard.

"But I want to get my car."

"I 'm afraid monsieur has no car."

"Eh?"

"They have all been taken for la patrie."

"You mean my machine has been confiscated?"

"Borrowed, perhaps. After the victory—" The guard shrugged his shoulders.

Monte shrugged his own shoulders. Then he laughed.

"After all," he said, "that is little enough to do for France. Inform the authorities they are welcome."

He saluted the guard, who returned the salute. Again he took Marjory's arm, and turned toward the hotel.

"There is nothing to do but to walk," he declared.

"Where?"

She could not understand his mood. It was as if this were a holiday instead of a very serious plight.

"Over the border. It is only some twenty-five miles. We can do it easily in two days; but even if it takes three—"

Even if it took a hundred, what did it matter, with her by his side? And by his side she must remain until her credit was restored. With only one louis d'or in her pocket, she was merely a woman, with all the limitations of her sex. She could not take to the open road alone. She did not have the physical strength that dictated the law for vagabonds. She must have a man near to fight for her, or it would go hard. Even Marie would be no protection in time of war.

Dumbly she followed his pace until they reached the hotel. The place was in confusion and the proprietor at his wits' end. In the midst of it, Monte was the only one apparently unmoved.

"Pack one small hand-bag," he ordered. "You must leave your trunks here."

"Yes, Monte," she submitted.

"I'll run back to the Roses, and meet you here in a half-hour. Will you be ready?"

"Yes. Marie will come with us, of course."

He shook his head.

"She must wait here until she can get to Paris. Find out if she has any cash."

"I want her to come with me," she pleaded.

"I doubt if she will want to come. Anyway, our fifty-five dollars won't stretch to her. We—we can't afford a maid."

She flushed at his use of "we." Nevertheless, what he said was true enough. That sum was a mere pittance. Fate had her in a tight grip.

"Be sure to bring your passport," he reminded her. "It is ten-thirty. I'll be here at eleven."

Hurrying back to his room, he took what he could crowd into his pockets: his safety razor and toothbrush, a few handkerchiefs and a change of socks. One did not need much on the open road. He carried his sweater—the old crimson sweater with the black "H"—more for her than for himself. The rest of his things he threw into his trunk and left in the care of the hotel.

She was waiting for him when he returned to the Hôtel d'Angleterre.

"You were right about Marie," she acknowledged. "She has two brothers in the army. She has money enough for her fare to Paris, and is going as soon as possible."

"In the meanwhile she is safe enough here. So, en avant!"

He took her bag, and they stepped out into the sunshine.

CHAPTER XXVIII
THE CORNICE ROAD

It was the Cornice Road that he followed—the broad white road that skirts the sea at the foot of the Alpes Maritimes. As far as Monte Carlo, he had walked it alone many the time. But he had never walked it with her, so it was a new road. It was a new world too, and as far as he was concerned there was no war. The blue sky overhead gave no hint of war; neither did the Mediterranean; neither did the trees full of singing birds; neither did the grasses and flowers: and these things, with the woman at his side, comprised, for the moment, his whole world. It was the world as originally created for man and woman. All that he was leaving behind—banks and hotels and taxis and servants and railroads—had nothing to do with the primal idea of creation. They were all extraneous. The heavens, the earth, the waters beneath the earth, man and woman created He them. That was all. That was enough.

Once or twice, alone in his camp in the Adirondacks, Monte had sensed this fact. With a bit of food to eat, a bit of tobacco to smoke in his old brier, a bit of ground to lie down upon at night, he had marveled that men found so many other things necessary to their comfort. But, after a week or two of that, he had always grown restless, and hurried back to New York and his club and his men servants. In turn he grew restless there, and hurried on to the still finer luxuries of the German liners and the Continent.

That was because he was lonesome—because she had not been with him. It was because—how clearly he saw it now!—he had never been complete by himself alone. He had been satisfying only half of himself. The other half he had tried to quiet with man-made things, with the artificial products of civilization. He had thought to allay that deep, undefined hunger in him with travel and sports and the attentions of hirelings. It had been easy at first; but, keen as nimble wits had been to keep pace with his desires with an ever-increasing variety of luxuries, he had exhausted them all within a decade and been left unsatisfied.

To-day it was as if with each intake of breath the sweet air reached for the first time the most remote corners of his lungs. He had never before had air enough. The sunshine reached to the marrow of his bones. Muscles that had lagged became vibrant. He could hardly keep his feet upon the ground. He would have liked to run; to keep on running mile after mile. He wondered when he would tire. He had a feeling that he could never tire. His back and arm muscles ached for action. He would have enjoyed a rough-and-tumble fight with some impudent fellow vagabond of the road.

Marjory walked by his side in silence. That was all he asked—simply that she should be there on the left, dependent upon him. Here was the nub of the matter. Always before she had been able to leave him if she wished. She had married him upon that condition. There had never been a moment, until now, when he had not been conscious of the fact that he was in no way necessary to her. The protection against Teddy and the others was merely a convenience. He had been able to save her from annoyance, that was all. At any time on that ride from Paris she could have left him and gone on her way quite safely. At Nice, that was just what she had done. It was to save her from the annoyance of himself that he had finally gone away. Had he been really needed, that would have been impossible. But he knew that she could get along without him as she did. Then when Peter had gone it was more because he needed her than because she needed him that he had returned. Down deep in his heart he knew that, whatever he may have pretended. She was safe enough from everything except possible annoyance. With plenty of gold at her command, there was nothing that he could buy for her that she could not buy for herself.

Now she had no gold—except one louis d'or. He was almost jealous of that single piece. He would have been glad if she lost it. If he had seen it drop from her bag, he would have let it lie where it fell.

She was merely a woman now. The muscles in her arms and legs were not strong. Because of that she could not leave his side, nor order him to leave. She must look to him to fight for her if fighting were necessary. She must look to him to put his strong arm about her and help her if she grew weary. She must look to him to provide her with food and shelter for the night. Physically she was like a child out here on the open road. But he was a man.

He was a man because he had something to protect. He was a man because he was responsible for some one besides himself. It was this that the other half of him had been craving all these years. It was this that completed him.

Yet his attitude toward her, in this respect, was strangely impersonal. He was looking for no reward. He did not consider that he was placing her in any way under an obligation to him. His joy in doing for her was not based upon any idea of furthering his own interests. He was utterly unselfish. He did not look ahead an hour. It was enough to have her here in a position where he could be of some service.

His love for her was another matter entirely. Whether she were with him or not, that would have remained the same. He loved her with all there was in him, and that was more or less distinct from any attitude that she might assume. It was a separate, definite, concrete fact, no longer open to argument—no longer to be affected by any of the petty accidents of circumstance. Not even she had now any control over it. It was within her power to satisfy it or not; but that was all. She could not destroy it. If she left it unfulfilled, then he must endure that, as Peter had. Peter was not sorry that he loved her, and Peter—why, Peter did not have the opportunity to sense more than the first faint beginnings of the word love. Peter had not had those weeks in Paris in which to get to know her; he had not had that wonderful ride through sunny France with Marjory by his side; and Peter had had nothing approaching such a day as this.

Monte turned to look at her. They had passed through Villefranche, and were now taking the up grade. The exercise had flushed her cheeks, giving her back the color she had lacked in the last few weeks. Her eyes were upon the ground, as if she did not dare raise them. Her face always seemed younger when one did not see the eyes. Asleep, she could not have looked over twenty. He marveled at how delicately feminine her forehead and nose were. And the lips—he could not look very long at her lips. Warm and full of curves, they tugged at his heart. They roused desire. Yet, had it been his blessed privilege to touch them with his own, he would have been very gentle about it. A man must needs always be gentle with her, he thought.

That was why he must not utter the phrases that burned within. It would only frighten her, and he must see that she was never frightened again. To himself he might say as much as he pleased, because she could not hear. He could repeat to himself over and over again, as he did now, "I love you—I love you—I love you."

Out loud, however, he said only:—

"Are you tired?"

She started even at that.

"No, Monte," she answered.

"We can rest any time you wish. We have all the time in the world ahead of us."

"Have we?"

"Days and weeks and months," he replied.

It was the old Monte she heard—the easy, care-free Monte. It made her feel easier.

"We should cross the border by to-morrow night, should n't we?" she asked.

"We could, if it were necessary," he admitted.

She quickened her pace unconsciously.

"I think we should get there as soon as possible."

"That," he said, "would be like hurrying through Eden."

She ventured to glance up at him. With his lean, strong face to the sun, his lithe body swinging rhythmically to his stride, he looked like an Indian chieftain. So he would have stalked through virgin forests. So, under different conditions, she might have been following his lead. But conditions were as they were. That is what she must keep in mind. He was here merely to escort her safely to Italy and to the steamer in which she was soon to sail for home. He was being decent to her, as under the same conditions he would be to any woman. He could scarcely do less than he was doing. She was forced upon him.

That he apparently took pleasure in the episode was natural enough. It was just the sort of experience he enjoyed. It was another pleasant excursion like the motor trip from Paris, with a touch of adventure added to give it spice. Possibly in his present mood there was also a trace of romance. Monte had his romantic side, based upon his quick sympathies. A maiden in distress was enough to rouse this. That was what happened yesterday when he told her of his love. He had been sincere enough for the moment, and no doubt believed everything he said. He had not given himself quite time enough to get back to his schedule. With that in good running order he would laugh at his present folly.

For she must remember that Monte had not as yet touched either the heights or the depths of love. It was in him to do that, but she must see to it that he did not. That was her task. Love as he saw it now was merely a pleasant garden, in May. It was a gypsy jaunt along the open road where it was pleasant enough to have her with him as he whistled along. A day or a week or a month or two of that was well enough, as he had said. Only she—she could not last that long. To-day and to-morrow at the utmost was as much as she could endure, with every minute a struggle to whip back her emotions. Were it safe, she would try to keep it up for his sake. If without danger she could keep him happy this way, not allowing him to go any further, she would try. But there is a limit to what of herself a woman may sacrifice, even if she is willing.

So, with her lips set, she stumbled along the Cornice Road by his side.

At five that evening they had made half their journey and stopped at a wayside inn—the inn of L'Agneau dansant. On a squeaking sign before the ancient stone structure, which looked as if it must have been there in the days of post-chaises, a frolicsome lamb danced upon his hind legs, smiling to all who paused there an invitation to join him in this innocent pastime and not take the world too seriously. The good humor of the crude painting appealed to Monte. He grinned back at L'Agneau dansant.

"I'm with you," he nodded.

Marjory, dusty and footsore, followed his gaze.

Then she too smiled.

"That fellow has the proper spirit," he declared. "Shall we place ourselves in his care?"

"I'm afraid I can't go any farther," she answered wearily.

Monsieur Soucin came out, looking to be in anything but the mood of the gay lamb before his door.

"Two rooms, a little supper, and some breakfast," explained Monte. "But we must strike a bargain. We are not American tourists—merely two travelers of the road without much gold and a long way to go."

"I have but a single louis d'or," put in madame.

"Monsieur! Madame!" interrupted Soucin. "I am sorry, but I cannot accommodate you at any price. In the next village a regiment of soldiers have arrived. I have had word that I must receive here ten officers. They come at seven to-night."

"But look here—madame is very tired," frowned Monte.

"I am sorry," answered Soucin helplessly.

Monte stepped nearer and jingled the gold in his pocket.

"Doubtless the next village in that case is without accommodations also," said Monte. "We will strike no bargain. Name your price up to ten louis d'or; for madame must rest."

Soucin shook his head.

"I am giving up my own room. I must sleep in the kitchen—if I sleep at all; which, mon Dieu, is doubtful."

"Supposing we had arrived yesterday, would you have turned us out to-night?"

"The inquiry was made how many rooms I had, and I answered truthfully."

Madame had sunk down on a bench by the door. Monte stared up the road and down the road. There was no other house in sight.

"You could not find a bed for madame even for ten louis d'or?"

"Not for a thousand, monsieur. If there are no beds, there are no beds."

Yet there was room enough thereabouts. Behind the inn an olive orchard extended up a gentle incline to a stone wall. Over this the sun was descending in a blaze of glory. A warm breeze stirred the dark leaves of the trees. A man could sleep out of doors on such a night as this. Monte turned again to the man.

"The orchard behind the house is yours?" he asked.

"Yes, monsieur."

"Then," said Monte, "if you will spare us a few blankets, madame and I will sleep there."

"Upon the ground?"

"Upon the blankets," smiled Monte.

"Ah, monsieur is from America!" exclaimed Soucin, as if that explained everything.

"Truly."

"And it is so the Indians sleep, I have read."

"You have read well. But we must have supper before the officers arrive. You can spare some bread and cheese?"

"I will do that."

"Then make it ready at once. And some coffee?"

"Yes, monsieur."

Monte returned to madame.

"I have engaged two rooms in the olive orchard," he announced.

CHAPTER XXIX
BENEATH THE STARS

The situation was absurd, but what could be done about it? France was at war, and there would be many who would sleep upon the ground who had never slept there before. Many, too, in the ground. Still, the situation was absurd—that Marjory, with all her thousands of dollars, should be forced to sleep out of doors. It gave her a startling sense of helplessness. She had been before in crowded places, but the securing of accommodations was merely a matter of increasing the size of her check. But here, even if one had a thousand louis d'or, that would have made no difference. Officers of the Army of France were not to be disturbed by the tinkle of gold. With a single gold-piece, moreover, one could not even make a tinkle.

She went into the inn to tidy herself before supper; but she hurried back to Monte as quickly as possible. Out of sight of him she felt as lost as a child in a forest. She had nothing to lean upon now but him. Without him here she would scarcely have had even identity. Her name, except as signed to a check, meant nothing. To have announced herself as Miss Marjory Stockton, or even as Madame Covington, would have left the soldiers of France merely smiling. To her sex they might have paid some deference, but to her sex alone. She was not anything except as she was attached to Monte—as a woman under the protection of her man.

This did not humble her. Her first clean, unguarded emotion was one of pride. Had it been her privilege to let herself go, she would have taken her place near him with her eyes afire—with her head held as proudly as any queen. Gladly would she have rested by his side in an olive orchard or a fisherman's hut or a forest or on the plains or anywhere fortune might take him. By his side—that would have been enough. If she were his woman and he her man, that would have been enough.

If she could only let herself go! As she came into the smoky old tavern room and he stepped forward to meet her, she swayed a little. He looked so big and wholesome and eager with his arms outstretched! They were alone here. It would have been so easy just to close her eyes and let her head rest against his shoulder—so easy and restful. He would have kissed her hair, and the ache would all have gone from her body and heart. He would draw her close and hold her tight—yes, for a day or two or a month or two. Then he would remember that week in which she had trifled with him, and he would hate her.

She pulled herself together.

"Is supper ready?"

It was such an inane remark! He turned aside like a boy who has been snubbed.

Monsieur Soucin had provided bread and cheese, a salad, and coffee. It was enough. She had no appetite. She took much more satisfaction in watching Monte and in pouring his coffee. His honest hunger was not disturbed by any vain speculations. He ate like a man, as he did everything like a man. It restored her confidence again.

"Soucin lent a mattress, which I have arranged just the other side of the wall. That is your room. With plenty of blankets you should be comfortable enough there," he said.

"And you?" she inquired.

"I am on this side of the wall," he replied gravely.

"What are you going to sleep upon?"

"A blanket."

If it had been possible to do so, she would have given him the mattress and slept upon the ground herself. That is what she would have liked to do.

"It's no more than I have done in the woods when I could n't make camp in time," he explained. "I had hoped to take you some day to my cabin near the lake."

She could think of nothing better than another inane remark:—

"It must be beautiful there."

He looked up.

"It always has been, but now—without you—"

"You must n't let me make any difference," she put in quickly.

"Why not?"

"Because you must n't. You must go on just as if you had never met me."

"Why?" He was as direct as a boy.

"Because that's best. Oh, I know, Monte. You must trust me to know what is good for you," she cried.

"I don't believe you know even what is good for yourself," he answered.

"I—I know what is right," she faltered.

He saw that he was disturbing her, and he did not want to do that.

"Perhaps in time we'll see," he said. "I have a notion that some day you and I will get straightened out."

"It does n't make so much difference about me; but you—you must get back to your schedule again as soon as ever you can."

"Perhaps to a new one; but that must include you."

She could not help the color in her cheeks. It was beyond her control.

"I must make my own little schedule," she insisted.

"You are going back to the farm?"

She nodded.

"To-morrow we shall be in Italy. Then a train to Genoa and the next boat," she said.

"After that?"

"In a week or so I shall be back where I started."

"Then?"

She laughed nervously.

"I can't think much ahead of that. Perhaps I shall raise chickens."

"Year after year?"

"Maybe."

"If you lived to be seventy you'd have a lot of chickens by then, would n't you?"

"I—I don't know."

It did sound ridiculous, the way he put it.

"Then—would you will them to some one?" he asked.

He was laughing at her. She was glad to have him do that rather than remain serious.

"Please don't make me look ahead to seventy," she shuddered.

Monsieur Soucin was hovering about nervously. He wished to have everything cleared away before the officers arrived, and they would be here now in half an hour. He was solicitous about madame.

"It is a great pity that madame should sleep out of doors," he said. "It makes my heart ache. But, with monsieur to guard her, at least madame will be safe."

Yes, safe from every one but herself. However, Monsieur Soucin could not be expected to read a lady's innermost thoughts. Indeed, it would scarcely have been gallant so to do.

"And now you wish to be rid of us," said Monte as he rose.

"Monsieur should not be unkind," sighed Soucin. "It is a necessity and not a wish."

"You have done as well as you could," Monte reassured him. "We shall probably rise early and be on our way before the soldiers, so—"

Monte slipped into his hand a gold-piece. It was too much from one point of view, and yet from another it was little enough. Soucin had unwittingly made an arrangement for which Monte could not pay in money.

"And my share?" inquired Marjory.

"One louis d'or," answered Monte unblushingly.

She fumbled in her bag and brought it out—the last she had. And Monte, in his reckless joy, handed that over also to Soucin. The man was too bewildered to do more than bow as he might before a prince and princess.

Monte led her up the incline through the heavy-leaved olive trees to her couch against the wall. It had been made up as neatly as in any hotel, with plenty of blankets and a pillow for her head.

"If you wish to retire at once," he said, "I'll go back to my side of the wall."

She hesitated. The wall was man-high and so thick that once he was behind it she would feel terribly alone.

"Or better still," he suggested, "you lie down and let me sit and smoke here. I'll be quiet."

It was a temptation she would have resisted had she not been so tired physically. As it was, half numbed with fatigue, she removed her hat and lay down between the blankets.

Monte slipped on his sweater with the black "H" and took a place against the wall at Marjory's feet.

"All comfy?" he asked.

"It's impossible to feel altogether comfortable when you're selfish," Marjory declared.

He took a thoughtful puff of his cigarette.

"I think you're right about that," he answered. "Only in this case there's no reason in the world for you to feel like that, because I'm comfortable too."

"Honestly?"

"Cross my heart. I'd rather be here than in the finest bed in Paris."

"You're so good," she murmured.

With all her muscles relaxed, and with him there, she felt as if she were floating in the clouds.

"It's strange you've always had that notion, because I'm not especially good," he replied. "Do you want to go to sleep, or may I talk a while longer?"

"Please to talk."

"Of course," he ran on meditatively, "something depends upon what you mean by being good. I used to think it was merely being decent. I've been that. It happened to be easy. But being good, as I see it now, is being good when it isn't easy—and then something more."

She was listening with bated breath, because he was voicing her own thoughts.

"It's being good to others besides yourself," he continued. "Forgetting yourself for them—when that is n't easy."

"Yes, it's that," she said.

"I don't want to boast," he said; "but, in a way, I come nearer being good at this moment, than ever before in my life."

"You mean because it's tiresome for you to sit there?"

"Because it's hard for me to sit here when I'd like to be kneeling by your side, kissing your hand, your forehead, your lips," he answered passionately.

She started to her elbow.

"I shan't move," he assured her. "But it is n't easy to sit here like a bump on a log with everything you're starving for within arm's reach."

"Monte!" she gasped. "Perhaps you'd better not talk."

"If it were only as easy to stop thinking!"

"Why don't one's thoughts mind?" she cried. "When they are told what's right, why don't they come right?"

"God knows," he answered. "I sit here and tell myself that if you don't love me I should let it go at that, and think the way I did before the solemn little pastor in Paris got so serious over what wasn't meant to be serious. I've tried, little woman. I tried hard when I left you with Peter. I could n't do it then, and I can't do it now. I hear over and over again the words the little minister spoke, and they grow more wonderful and fine every day. I think he must have known then that I loved you or he would not have uttered them."

The leaves in the olive trees rustled beneath the stars.

"Dear wife," he cried, "when are you coming to me?"

He did not move. She saw his broad shoulders against the wall. She saw his arms folded over his chest as if to keep them tight. She saw his clenched lips.

"God help me to keep silent," she prayed.

"When are you coming?" he repeated wearily. "Will it be one year or two years or three years?"

She moistened her lips. He seemed to speak as though it were only a matter of time—as though it were he who was being punished and it was only a question of how long. She sank back with her eyes upon the stars darting shafts of white light through the purple.

"And what am I going to do while I'm waiting?" he went on, as though to himself.

Grimly she forced out the words:—

"You—you must n't wait. There 's nothing to wait for."

She saw his arms tighten; saw his lips grow hard.

"Nothing?" he exclaimed. "Don't make me believe that, because—then there would n't be anything."

She grew suddenly afraid.

"There would be everything else in the world for you—everything except me," she trembled. "And I count for so little. That's what I want you to learn. That's what, in a little while, you will learn. That's what you must learn. If you'll only hold on until to-morrow—until the next day and I'm gone—"

"Gone?"

He sprang to his feet.

"Monte!" she warned.

In terror she struggled to her own feet. The white light of the stars bathed their faces. In the distance he heard the notes of a trumpet sounding taps. It roused him further. It was as though the night were closing in upon him—as though life were closing in on him.

He turned and seized her.

"Marjory!" he cried. "Look me in the eyes."

She obeyed.

"They are sounding taps over there," he panted. "Before they are through—do you love me, Marjory?"

Never before in all his life had he asked her that directly. Always she had been able to avoid the direct answer. Now—

She tried to struggle free.

"Don't—don't ask me that!" she pleaded.

"Before they are through—do you love me?"

Piercing the still night air the final notes came to her. There was no escape. Either she must lie or tell the truth and to lie—that meant death.

"Quick!" he cried.

"I do!" she whispered.

"Then—"

He tried to draw her to him.

"You made me tell you, Monte," she sobbed. "Oh, you made me tell the truth."

"The truth," he nodded with a smile; "that was all that was necessary. It's all that is ever necessary."

He had released her. She was crowding against the wall. She looked up at him.

"Now," he said, "if it's one year or two years or three years—what's the difference?"

Her eyes suddenly grew as brilliant as the stars. She straightened herself.

"Then," she trembled, "if it's like that—"

"It might as well be now," he pleaded.

Unsteadily, like one walking in a dream, she tottered toward him. He caught her in his arms and kissed her lips—there in the starlight, there in the olive orchard, there in the Garden of Eden.

THE END

Milton Keynes UK
Ingram Content Group UK Ltd.
UKHW030740071024
449371UK00006B/687